PhotoPlus X6 User Guide

D0805284

Contents

1 Welcome

Welcome

Welcome to **PhotoPlus X6** from **Serif**—more than ever, the best value in image creation and editing software for any home, school, organization, or growing business. PhotoPlus is the number one choice for working with photographs and paint-type images, whether for the web, multimedia, or the printed page.

PhotoPlus has the features you'll need... from importing or creating pictures, through manipulating colours, making image adjustments, applying filter effects and so much more, all the way to final export. Built-in support for the most modern digital cameras makes it easy to open your very own digital photos, either as JPG or as unprocessed raw images.

PhotoPlus also offers on-computer post-shoot development, using **Import Raw**, where you're in full control of your raw image's white balance and exposure, and perform "blown" highlight recovery. For image adjustments, filter effects (including stunning artistic effects), or layer cutouts, try **PhotoFix**, **Filter Gallery**, and **Cutout Studio**, respectively.

PhotoPlus and PhotoPlus Organizer: a powerful combination

PhotoPlus takes care of all your image creation and photo editing needs. However, if you're looking to take a step back from photo editing and manage your collection of photos, scanned images, etc. you can use PhotoPlus Organizer. This is installed automatically with PhotoPlus, and offers a powerful platform for launching your photos in PhotoPlus. You'll be able to sort, group, rate, and tag your photos, as well as filter your photos for display by several methods.

Registration

Don't forget to register your new copy, using the **Registration Wizard** on the **Help** menu. That way, we can keep you informed of new developments and future upgrades!

New features

- **64-bit Operation for Faster Photo Editing**
  PhotoPlus X6 is fully optimized for operation on 64-bit computers, and will automatically install for 64-bit operation accordingly. Open photos of large image size, especially raw images, in an instant! Benefit from all-round faster PhotoPlus performance.

- **Intelligent Brush-based Selection**
  Use the **Smart Selection Brush Tool** to create fast accurate selections which intelligently grow to objects and edges in your image. Improve an existing selection by using smart edge refinement to perfect the selection boundary.

- **Improved Raw Image Control**
  Use Import Raw dialog for faster image loading and convenient in-place photo adjustments: more powerful Lighting and Noise Reduction adjustments; new Curves, HSL, Lens Distortion, Lens Vignette, Black and White Film, and Unsharp Mask adjustments are available. Use masks to selectively control areas subject to adjustment. The Import Raw dialog also hosts Red-eye, Spot-repair, and Crop tools for photo retouching.

- **Tilt-Shift Effects for Miniature Scenes**
  The **Depth of Field** filter hosts the new Tilt-shift effect. Simulate miniature scenes by targeting an area of focus and controlling the extent of blurring, e.g. in the photo foreground and background.

- **Fill Layers for Creative Colour Effects**
  For ease of use, editable fill layers take a solid or gradient fill (Linear, Radial, Conical, or Square) without the need to define a selection or shaped region to fill in advance. With opacity adjustment as well as fill control you'll be able to create semi-transparent colour layers or solid-fill backgrounds with ease. For more creativity, try applying blend modes to fill layers.

- **Vector Masks for Versatile Drawn Mask Control**
  Create vector masks that give you fully editable smooth curves for masking on standard or adjustment layers.

- **Latest Noise Reduction Technology**
  Remove noise from photos taken in low-light conditions or at high
  ISO camera settings with the new **Noise Reduction** filter. Available via
  RAW import or PhotoFix, both **luma** and **chroma noise** can be
  removed using independent controls.

- **Non-destructive Cropping**
  Enjoy the ability to uncrop any previously cropped images at any time
  in the future. Ideal if you want to re-crop your image again or if you
  change your mind about the original crop.

- **Increased Zoom Range**
  The PhotoPlus zoom range has been doubled to improve detailed
  editing of large images or icon creation.

- **Sub-pixel Guides for Vector Drawing**
  Fine positioning of guides to the sub-pixel level lets you accurately
  position lines, shapes, QuickShapes, and paths.

- **Enhanced Export Optimizer**
  Easier than ever exporting is possible! As well as panning your export
  preview by default, you can export as TIF, WDP, or PNG using bit
  depths of 48 bit or 64 bit. CMYK or MONO (8 or 16bps) export
  options are also available. EXIF/IPTC information can be retained or
  discarded on export.

Installation

Minimum:

- Windows-based PC with DVD/CD drive and mouse

- Operating system:
  Microsoft Windows® XP* SP2 (32 bit)
  Windows® Vista (32 or 64 bit)
  Windows® 7 (32 or 64 bit)
  Windows® 8 (32 or 64 bit)

- 512MB RAM (1GB RAM for 64-bit operation)

- 821MB free hard disk space (including PhotoPlus Organizer).

- 1024 x 768 monitor resolution

Additional disk resources and memory are required when editing large and/or complex images.

* Requires Microsoft Windows Imaging Component.

Optional:

- Windows-compatible printer

- Pen (graphics) tablet

- Internet account and connection required for product updates and accessing online resources

Installation procedure

- Insert your purchased disc into your disc drive.

  - If AutoPlay is enabled on the drive, this automatically starts the Setup Wizard. Follow the on-screen instructions for install.
    OR

  - If AutoPlay is not enabled (or doesn't start the install automatically), navigate to your program disc and double-click **autorun.exe**.

 32 or 64-bit PhotoPlus X6 installs to respective 32 or 64-bit computers.

2 Getting Started

Startup Wizard

Once PhotoPlus has been installed, you're ready to start!

- For Windows Vista/7: The Setup routine during install adds a **Serif PhotoPlus X6** entry to the Windows Start menu. Use the Windows **Start** button to pop up the Start Menu, click on **All Programs** and then click the PhotoPlus icon.

- For Windows 8: The Setup routine during install adds a **Serif PhotoPlus X6** entry to the desktop. Use the Windows **Start** button to pop up the desktop, and then click the PhotoPlus icon.

On program launch, the Startup Wizard is displayed which offers different routes into PhotoPlus:

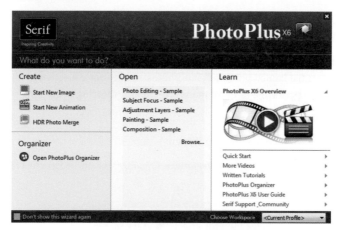

- **Start New Image**, to start from scratch.

- **Start New Animation**, to create an animated GIF.

- **HDR Photo Merge**, for bracketing photos taken at different exposure levels.

- **Open PhotoPlus Organizer**, to manage and filter photos for PhotoPlus.

- **Open**, lists recently opened photos and PhotoPlus projects. Hover over each entry for a quick preview!

- **Learn**, to access online tutorial resources.

Use the **Choose Workspace** drop-down list to choose your workspace appearance (i.e., Studio tab positions, tab sizes, and show/hide tab status). You can adopt the default workspace profile <**Default Profile**>, the last used profile <**Current Profile**>, a range of pre-defined profiles, or a custom workspace profile you've previously saved.

 As you click on different profiles from the menu, your workspace will preview each tab layout in turn.

If you don't want to use the Startup Wizard again, check the "Don't show this wizard again" box. However, we suggest you leave it unchecked until you're familiar with the equivalent PhotoPlus commands. Switch the wizard back on again by checking **Use Startup Wizard** via **Preferences**. (General menu option) on the **File** menu.

Organizing photos

PhotoPlus Organizer is Serif's powerful photo management application which acts as an essential launch point for your photos. From your collection of photos you'll be able to perform a range of **management** and **filtering** operations.

To launch Organizer:

1. Display PhotoPlus's Startup Wizard.

2. Select **Open PhotoPlus Organizer**. Organizer is launched as a separate application.
    OR

    From the **Standard** toolbar, select **Organizer**.
    OR
    From the **File** menu, select **Organizer**.

 Press your **F1** key to view PhotoPlus Organizer Help.

PhotoPlus Organizer is a great starting point for editing photos in PhotoPlus. Click **Edit in PhotoPlus** on the top toolbar to open, then edit, your chosen photo in PhotoPlus.

Starting from scratch

PhotoPlus deals with two basic kinds of image files. We'll differentiate them as **pictures** (still images) and **animations** (moving images). The two types are closely related, and creating either from scratch in PhotoPlus involves the same series of steps.

PhotoPlus lets you create an image based on a pre-defined canvas size (e.g., 10 x 8 in). Different canvas size options are available from a range of categories (International/US Paper, Photo, Video, Web, or Animation). Alternatively, you can create your own custom canvas sizes, and even store them for future use. For either preset or custom sizes, the resolution can be set independently of canvas size.

When you create a new image, you can choose to work in different colour modes, i.e. RGB or Greyscale, in either 8- or 16-bits/channel. Use a **Bit Depth** of 16 bit for higher levels of image detail.

To create a new image or animation (using Startup Wizard):

1. The first time you launch PhotoPlus, you'll see the **Startup Wizard**, with a menu of choices. Click **Start New Image** or **Start New Animation**.

2. In the New Image dialog, you can either:

    1. For a **preset** canvas size, select a suitable **Category** from the drop-down list. Categories are named according to how your image or animation is intended to be used, e.g. pick a Photo category for photo-sized canvases.

    2. Pick a canvas **Size** from the drop-down list.
        OR

    •   For a custom canvas size, enter your own **Width** and **Height**. If the dimensions are non-standard, the Size drop-down list will be shown as "Custom." For future use, save the custom size with

        Add Size (from the ▽ button) if necessary.

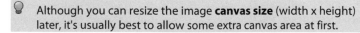
Although you can resize the image **canvas size** (width x height) later, it's usually best to allow some extra canvas area at first.

3. (Optional) Add a **Resolution** for the new image file. Leave the resolution as it is unless you're sure a different value is required.

4. (Optional) Select a **Colour Mode**, choosing to operate in RGB or Greyscale mode.

5. (Optional) Select a **Bit Depth** of 16 bits per channel for projects which require higher levels of colour detail. Otherwise a bit depth of 8 bits/channel is used as default.

6. (Optional) Select a background type in the **Background** drop-down list.

    *   When painting from scratch, you'll normally choose White.

    *   You can also choose Background Colour, to use the current background colour shown on the Colour tab.

    *   When creating an animation, Transparent is often called for.

7. When you've made your selections, click **OK.**

To create a new picture or animation (during your session):

1. Click ⬜ **New** on the **Standard** toolbar. This will open the Startup Wizard (see p. 9) or the New Image dialog (if the Startup Wizard is disabled).

2. In the New Image dialog, set your canvas size (see p. 11) and then check **Animation** to create an animation or leave unchecked for a picture.

3. Click **OK**. The new image or animation opens in a separate untitled window.

Opening an existing file

You can use the Startup Wizard to access files recently viewed in PhotoPlus or any file on your computer. PhotoPlus opens all the standard formats for print and web graphics, in addition to its native SPP format, Adobe Photoshop (PSD) files, and Paint Shop Pro (PSP) files.

Raw files open in an Import Raw dialog, which offers image adjustment on the "undeveloped" image before opening. See Adjusting raw images in PhotoPlus Help. Similarly, intermediate HDR images (OpenEXR and Radiance) can be opened in a dialog at any time for readjusting your HDR merge results (see p. 74).

To open a recently opened PhotoPlus Picture or graphic (via Startup Wizard):

1. From the Startup Wizard (at startup time or via **File>New from Startup Wizard**.), select your SPP file or graphic file from the **Open** section. The most recently opened file will be shown at the top of the list. To see a thumbnail preview of any file before opening, hover over its name in the list.

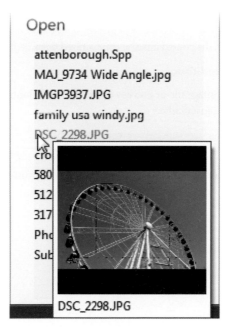

2. Click the file name to open it.

PhotoPlus opens the image as a maximized currently active document; the document appears in the Documents tab.

 Recently viewed files also appear at the bottom of the **File** menu. Simply select the file name to open it.

To open any image file:

1. From the Startup Wizard (at startup time or via **File>New from Startup Wizard**.), click **Browse**.
   OR

   Click **Open** on the **Standard** toolbar.

2. In the Open dialog, select the folder and file name. To open multiple files, press the **Shift** or **Ctrl** key when selecting their names (for adjacent or non-adjacent files).

3. Click **Open** to open the desired image as a maximized document.

To open images by drag-and-drop:

- Drag and drop an image file or preview thumbnail into PhotoPlus from Windows Explorer either:

  - into the current workspace (to create a new layer).
    OR

  - onto the Documents tab (to create a new image window).

Saving a file

The process of **saving** differs depending on the type of file you are working on, the file's current saved state and the file type you want to save.

PhotoPlus lets you work on (and save) one of several file types:

- An open **PhotoPlus Picture** (**.spp**) file is project-based and so preserves 'project' information (e.g., layers, masks, paths) when saving the file.

- For a currently open **image** file you can edit and save the image back to its original format. However, if you've added layers, masks, or paths to your image you'll be prompted to optionally create an spp file to preserve 'project' information (otherwise it will be lost). If you choose not to create an spp file, the additional content is included in the now flattened image.

- An intermediate **HDR** image can be saved, which stores the results of an HDR Photo Merge in an HDR file for future use. See Merging bracketed photos on p. 74 for more information.

To save your PhotoPlus Picture (.spp):

- Click the 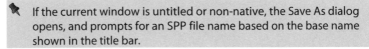 **Save** button on the **Standard** toolbar.
  OR
  To save under a different path or base name, choose **Save As** from the **File** menu. The window title bar is updated accordingly.

> ✎ If the current window is untitled or non-native, the Save As dialog opens, and prompts for an SPP file name based on the base name shown in the title bar.

The procedure for an altered image is slightly more complicated as PhotoPlus will assist you in deciding if you want to save or lose any added "project information" added to the original image.

To save your currently open image:

- If you've altered the background layer only and no layers, paths, or masks have been added, you can save (without prompt) the altered image to its current base name (shown in the window title bar) by choosing one of the above **Save** options. Changes are included in the image.

  OR

- If you've added layers, paths, or masks to your image, when you click a **Save** option you'll be asked if you want to preserve the "project" information.

    - In the dialog, click **Yes** to save your project information (as an SPP file).

      OR

      Click **No** to save as a flattened image (i.e., without layers).

To revert an image file:

- Click **Revert** from the **File** menu. The last saved version of your image is displayed.

3 Layers, Masks, and Blending

Introduction to layers

If you're accustomed to thinking of pictures as flat illustrations in books, or as photographic prints, the concept of **image layers** may take some getting used to. However, they are one of the most powerful features in PhotoPlus, allowing you to adjust and manipulate your photos in a variety of ways in a non-destructive environment.

Think of layers as transparent sheets upon which you can add adjustments, filters, paint colours, and add further images, shapes, and text to build up the perfect picture.

Kinds of layers

In a typical PhotoPlus image—for example, a photograph you've scanned in, a new picture file you've just created, or a standard bitmap file you've opened—there is one layer that behaves like a conventional "flat" image. This is called the **Background layer**, and you can think of it as having paint overlaid on an opaque, solid colour surface.

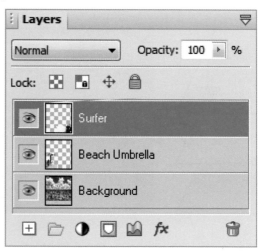

You can create any number of new layers in your image. Each new one appears on top of the currently active layer, comprising a stack that you can view and manipulate with the Layers tab.

We call these additional layers **standard layers** to differentiate them from the Background layer. Standard layers behave like transparent sheets through which the underlying layers are visible.

In the example above, the standard layer 'Surfer' is highest in the stack, followed by 'Beach Umbrella'. The Background layer contains the beach, sea and sky photo.

Other types of layers also exist in PhotoPlus:

- **Shape layers** are specifically designed to keep drawn lines and shapes (including QuickShapes) separate from the other layers so that they remain editable. (See Drawing and editing lines and shapes; p. 142.)

- **Text layers** work like Shape layers, but are intended exclusively for text. (See Creating and editing text; p. 150.)

- **Fill layers** contain an adjustable solid colour or gradient fill. (See Fill Layers; PhotoPlus Help.)

- **Adjustment layers** apply corrective image adjustments to lower layers. (See Using adjustment layers; p. 38.)

- **Filter layers**, are much like standard layers, but you can apply one or more filter effects to the layer without permanently altering layer content. You also have full control over effects in the future. (See Using filter layers; p. 58.)

For now though we're concerned mainly with the Background and standard layers.

A key distinction is that pixels on the Background layer are always opaque, while those on standard layers can vary in opacity (or transparency—another way of expressing the same property). That's because standard layers have a "master" Opacity setting that you can change at any time (with on-screen real-time preview), while the Background layer does not. A couple of examples will show how this rule is applied in PhotoPlus:

- Suppose you are creating a new image. The New Image dialog provides three choices for Background: White, Background Colour, and Transparent. If you pick White or Background Colour, the Layers tab shows a single layer in the new image named "Background". If you pick Transparent, however, the single layer is named "Layer 1"—and in this case, the image has no Background layer.

- If you cut, delete, or move a selection on the Background layer, the "hole" that's left exposes the current background colour as shown on the Colour tab (illustrated below on the left). The same operations on a standard layer exposes a transparent hole (illustrated below on the right).

Selections and layers

With few exceptions, you will work on just one layer at any given time—click a layer on the Layers tab to activate and work on that layer. Tools and commands generally affect the entire active layer. However, if there's a selection in place, tools and commands are limited to the pixels inside the selection.

Selections are independent from layers. They don't actually include image content—they just describe a region with boundaries. Therefore, if your image has multiple layers and you switch to another layer, the selection stays in place and follows you to the new active layer.

Operations involving layers

Many standard operations, such as painting, selecting and moving, Clipboard actions, adjusting colours, applying effects, and so on, are possible on both the Background layer and standard layers.

Others, such as rearranging the order of layers in the stack, setting up different colour interactions (blend modes and blend ranges) between layers, varying layer opacity (transparency), applying 2D layer effects and 3D layer effects, using depth maps, creating animation frames, or masking, only work with standard layers.

Once an image has more than just a background layer, the layer information can only be preserved by saving the image in the native PhotoPlus (.spp) format. Multiple layers are **merged** when you export an image to a standard "flat" bitmap format (e.g., .png). It's best to save your work-in-progress as SPP files, and only export to a different file format as the final step. (See Saving a file and Exporting to another file format on p. 15 and 164, respectively.)

Some standard operations can be applied to all layers simultaneously by checking the **Use All Layers** option from the context toolbar.

To carry out basic layer operations:

- To select a layer, click on its name in the Layers tab. The selected layer is now the **active layer**. Note that each layer's entry includes a preview thumbnail, which is visible at all times and is especially useful when identifying layer contents.

- ⊞ To create a new standard layer above the active layer, click the **New Layer** button on the Layers tab. Dragging a file from Windows Explorer and dropping it onto the current window also creates a new layer from the dragged image.

- ◑ Click the **New Fill or Adjustment Layer** button to apply a **Fill Layer** or an image adjustment layer. (See Fill Layers in PhotoPlus Help and Using adjustment layers on p. 38.)

- ▢ The **Add Layer Mask** button adds a mask to the currently selected layer. (See Importance of Masks in PhotoPlus Help and Using masks on p. 27.)

- The **Add Layer Depth Map** button creates a depth map for the selected layer. (See Using depth maps in PhotoPlus Help.)

- *fx* The **Add Layer Effects** button creates a 2D or 3D effect on the layer. Right-click to copy/paste, clear or hide effects.

- 👁 To make a layer's contents visible or invisible, click the **Hide/Show Layer** button next to its name on the Layers tab.

- To convert any shape, text or fill layer to a standard layer, right-click on the layer name and choose **Rasterize** from the menu.

- To convert the Background layer to a standard layer (which supports transparency), right-click "Background" on the Layers tab and choose **Promote to Layer**. The layer's name changes from "Background" to "Layer <number>." To convert a standard layer to a Background layer, right-click the layer and choose **Layer to Background**.

- To convert the layer to a non-destructive filter layer, for applying and managing effect and adjustment filters, right-click and select **Convert to Filter Layer**. (See Using filter layers in PhotoPlus Help.)

- To access Layer Properties—including Name, Blend Mode, Opacity, and Blend Ranges—right-click the layer name and choose **Properties**.

To control layer content:

- To select all layer content use **Select>Select All** or **Ctrl+A**. To select non-transparent regions on a layer, **Ctrl**-click on a layer thumbnail. Use **Select>Invert** or **Ctrl+Shift+I** to select transparent regions.

- To move layer content, select one or more layers containing the content to be moved (from the Layers tab), then drag with the **Move Tool** with no selection area present (press **Ctrl+D** to remove any selection).

- To align layer content, select one or more layers (as above), then choose **Align** from the **Layers** menu, then select an option from the submenu.

- To distribute layer content, select one or more layers (as above), then choose **Distribute** from the **Layers** menu, then select an option from the submenu.

Adjusting opacity/transparency

Opacity and **transparency** describe essentially the same thing. They both describe the extent to which a particular pixel's colour contributes to the overall colour at that point in the image. Fully opaque pixels contribute their full colour value to the image. Fully transparent pixels are invisible: they contribute nothing to the image. In-between pixels are called semi-transparent.

Fully opaque text   *Semi-transparent text*
(100% Opacity)   *(50% Opacity)*

You'll primarily encounter opacity in one of these two contexts:

- As a property of the pixels laid down by individual **tools** (Paintbrush, Clone, Eraser, Fill, Smudge, QuickShape, and more).
  The map of opacity values for all the pixels on a particular layer is stored along with the layer and is known as its

- As a property of individual **standard layers** (in example above). The layer's opacity setting affects all the pixels on the layer, and is cumulative with the opacity of individual pixels already there.

To set a tool's opacity:

• Select the tool (e.g., Paintbrush Tool) and from the context toolbar either enter a percentage **Opacity** value directly or use the slider (click the option's right arrow button).

To set a layer's opacity:

• Select the layer in the Layers tab and adjust the **Opacity** setting at the top of the tab—either enter a percentage **Opacity** value directly or use the slider (click the option's right arrow button).

To read the opacity values of pixels on all visible layers:

1. Select the **Colour Pickup Tool** from the **Tools** toolbar and move it around the image.

2. Read the value shown for "O" (Opacity) on the Hintline (e.g., O:60%).

RGB: 67 255 94 O:60%

The readout updates constantly, showing the opacity value of each pixel under the cursor.

For more useful hints and tips about using opacity, see PhotoPlus Help.

Using masks

Masking can also be applied to adjustment and effect filters, where you can isolate regions (e.g., an image background) to which you want a filter to be applied. (See Using filter layers on p. 58). Similarly, you can use studio-based filter masking on adjustments by using PhotoFix (see p. 46).

Creating the mask

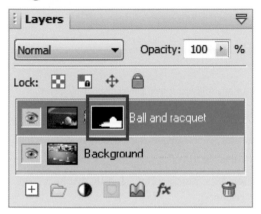

Before you can use a mask, you have to create it on a particular layer. The mask can start out as transparent (revealing the whole layer), opaque (hiding the whole layer), or—if you create it from a selection (opposite)—a bit of both (with only the selected region hidden or revealed). The mask shows as a mask thumbnail.

The choice depends on how you want to work with the layer's contents. By darkening portions of a clear mask, you can selectively fade layer pixels. By lightening an opaque mask, you selectively reveal layer pixels.

To create a mask:

1. Select a layer in the Layers tab. This is the layer where you want to create the mask, and select specific region(s) if desired.

2. Click the **Add Layer Mask** button to create a Reveal All mask (or Reveal Selection if there is one). Instead, **Alt**-click the button for a Hide All Mask (or Hide Selection).

    OR

    Choose **Mask>Add Mask** from the **Layers** menu and then one of the following from the submenu:

    *   **Reveal All** for a transparent mask over the whole layer

    *   **Hide All** for an opaque mask over the whole layer

    *   **Reveal Selection** for an opaque mask with transparent "holes" over the selected region(s)

    *   **Hide Selection** for a transparent mask with opaque "blocks" over the selected region(s)

On the Layers tab, a mask preview thumbnail appears, confirming that a mask exists.

Editing on the mask

When you create your mask you immediately enter Edit Mask mode, where you can use the full range of painting tools, selection options, flood fills, gradient fills, and effects to alter the mask's greyscale values. These manipulations cause corresponding changes in opacity, which in turn changes the appearance of the pixels on the layer itself.

The image window's titlebar shows "**Mask**", indicating that a mask is currently being edited. The Colour tab switches to Greyscale mode when you're editing a mask, and reverts to the previous setting when you exit Edit Mask mode. This means anything you paste from the Clipboard onto the mask will automatically be converted to greyscale.

 As long as you are editing the mask, you're only seeing a preview of changes on the layer.

You can switch out of Edit Mask mode at any time to edit the active layer directly (or any other part of the image), then switch back to resume work on the mask.

To edit the active layer:

- Click the layer thumbnail to the left of the Mask thumbnail. The thumbnail is then bordered in white.

To edit the active layer's mask:

- Click the mask thumbnail.

In Edit Mask mode, you're normally viewing not the mask, but rather the effects of changes "as if" you were making them on the layer below. Adding a Reveal All mask can be a bit confusing, because there's initially no evidence the mask is there at all (i.e. the layer appears exactly the same as it did before you added the mask)!

It's sometimes helpful to switch on the **View Mask** setting, which hides the layer and lets you see **only** the mask, in all its greyscale glory. For example, a Reveal All mask appears pure white in View Mask mode—the white represents a clear mask with no effect on the underlying layer pixels' opacity. View Mask can also be useful in the latter stages of working on a mask, to locate any small regions that may have escaped your attention.

To view the active layer's mask:

- **Alt**-click the mask thumbnail, to display the mask in black and white. **Alt**-click a second time to view the mask as a tinted overlay.

    To stop viewing the mask, click on the layer thumbnail.

White or light portions of the mask reveal layer pixels (make them more opaque). Black or dark portions hide layer pixels (making them more transparent).

You can **disable** the mask to see how the layer looks without the mask's effects. Note that disabling the mask is not the same as cancelling Edit Mask mode—it only affects your view of the layer, not which plane (i.e. mask or layer) you're working on.

To disable the active layer's mask:

- **Shift**-click the mask preview thumbnail. (**Shift**-click again to enable masking again.)

     When the mask is disabled, a red "X" appears across its thumbnail.

If you want to fine-tune a mask or layer's position independently of each other it's possible to **unlink** them. You may have noticed a small link button between the layer and mask thumbnails on the Layers tab, i.e.

A click on this ⫿ button will unlink the layer and mask, changing the button to display a red cross through it (⫿). By selecting the layer or mask thumbnail, you can then drag the layer or mask on the page, respectively. After fine-tuning, click the button to relink the mask to the layer.

Using blend modes

You can think of **blend modes** as different rules for putting pixels together to create a resulting colour. In PhotoPlus, you'll encounter blend modes on layers or effects. The colours of an upper layer blend with colours of the lower layer in different ways according to the upper layer's blend mode.

To set a tool's blend mode:

- Select the tool and use the drop-down list (displays Normal by default) on the tool's context toolbar.

To set a standard layer's blend mode:

- On the Layers tab, select the layer and choose the mode from the blend mode's drop-down list.

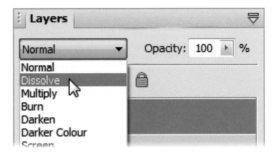

It's also possible to include or exclude tones or colours to be included in any blending operation by using **blend ranges**. For more details, see Using blend ranges in PhotoPlus Help.

A tool or layer's **Opacity** setting interacts with its blend mode to produce varying results. For details, see Adjusting opacity/transparency on p. 25.

4 Making Image Adjustments

Introduction to image adjustments

A major part of photo-editing is making corrections (i.e., **adjustments**) to your own near-perfect images. Whether you've been snapping with your digital camera or you've just scanned a photograph, at some point you may need to call on PhotoPlus's powerful photo-correction tools to fix some unforeseen problems.

For photo-correction, several methods can be adopted. You can use a combination of:

- **Image colour adjustments**: For applying colour adjustments to a selection or layers.

- **PhotoFix**: For making cumulative corrective adjustments from within a studio environment.

- **Retouch** brush-based tools: Red Eye, Smudge, Blur, Sharpen, Dodge/Burn (for exposure control), Sponge (for saturation control), Scratch Remover.

If you work with raw images you can make image adjustments on your unprocessed raw file (before interpolation). Adjustments include **white balance**, **exposure**, **highlight recovery**, **noise reduction**, and **chromatic aberration** removal. See Adjusting raw images in PhotoPlus Help.

Overview: Adjusting image colours

PhotoPlus provides a number of different adjustment filters that you can apply to a selection or to an active standard layer. Typically, these adjustments are used to correct deficiencies in the original image.

The adjustment can be applied in one of several ways:

- via the **Adjustments tab**, as an **adjustment layer** (non-destructive).

- via **PhotoFix**, a studio environment for managing and applying cumulative adjustments (non-destructive).

- via **Image>Adjust**, on a filter layer (non-destructive).

- via **Image>Adjust**, on a standard layer (destructive).

Here's a summary of the available PhotoPlus image adjustments:

- **Levels**: Displays a histogram plot of lightness values in the image, from which you can adjust the tonal range by shifting dark, light, and gamma values.

- **Curves**: Displays lightness values in the image using a line graph, and lets you adjust points along the curve to fine-tune the tonal range.

- **Brightness/Contrast**: Brightness refers to overall lightness or darkness, while contrast describes the tonal range, or spread between lightest and darkest values.

- **Shadow/Highlight/Midtone**: Controls the extent of shadows, highlights, and contrast within the image.

- **Hue/Saturation/Lightness**: Hue refers to the colour's tint—what most of us think of as rainbow or spectrum colours with name associations, like "blue" or "magenta". Saturation describes the colour's purity—a totally unsaturated image has only greys. Lightness is what we intuitively understand as relative darkness or lightness—ranging from full black at one end to full white at the other.

- **Colourize**: Lets you recolour an image using Hue, Saturation, and Lightness.

- **Vibrance**: Boosts low-saturation colours in your image, while high-saturation colours are less affected.

- **Colour Balance**: Lets you adjust colour and tonal balance for general colour correction in the image.

- **Replace Colour**: Tags one or more ranges of the full colour spectrum that require adjustment in the image, then apply variations in hue, saturation, and/or brightness to just those colour regions (not to be confused with the simpler Replace Colour Tool).

- **Selective Colour**: Lets you add or subtract a certain percentage of cyan, magenta, yellow, and/or black ink for creating effects.

- **Channel Mixer**: Modifies a colour channel using a mix of the current colour channels.

- **Gradient Map**: Lets you remap greyscale (lightness) information in the image to a selected gradient. The function replaces pixels of a given lightness in the original image with the corresponding colour value from the gradient spectrum.

- **Lens Filter**: Adjusts the colour balance for warming or cooling down your photos. It digitally mimics the placement of a filter on the front of your camera lens.

- **Black and White Film**: Used for greyscale conversion with controllable source channel input.

- **Threshold**: Creates a monochromatic (black and white) rendering. You can set the threshold, i.e. the lightness or grey value above which colours are inverted.

- **Equalize**: Evenly distributes the lightness levels between existing bottom (darkest) and top (lightest) values.

- **Negative Image**: Inverts the colours, giving the effect of a photographic negative.

- **Clarity**: Lets you sharpen up your photos using local contrast.

- **Posterize**: Produces a special effect by reducing the image to a limited number of colours.

Instead of the manual tonal adjustments above, the PhotoPlus **Image** menu affords a number of functions you can apply to correct shadow/highlight values in an image automatically. **Adjust>AutoLevels** or **Adjust>AutoContrast** may do the job in one go; if not, you can use **Adjust>Levels**. or **Adjust>Shadow/Highlight/Midtone**. (See PhotoPlus Help for details.)

 Use the Histogram tab to display statistics and image colour values, helping you to evaluate the kinds of image adjustments that may be needed.

Using adjustment layers

Adjustment layers are recommended for applying image adjustments experimentally and non-destructively to your image.

The Adjustments tab lists available adjustments in a selectable adjustments list; after selection, the tab displays a Settings pane for that adjustment (and for any selected adjustment layer present in the Layers tab).

An adjustment layer is created by selecting an adjustment from the **Adjustments tab**. As its name suggests, an adjustment layer is considered a layer so it will appear in the Layers tab on creation.

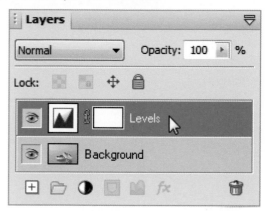

Unlike the other layer types, adjustment layers don't store content in the form of bitmap images, text, or shapes. Rather, an adjustment layer applies the adjustment to content on **all** layers below it (although you can restrict the effects of the adjustment by adding to a group or by clipping to the immediate layer below).

The layer is essentially a container in which only the adjustment's settings and its layer properties are stored.

You can drag an adjustment layer up or down within the list to determine exactly which other layers are below and therefore affected by it.

Adjustment layers let you revisit the settings for a given adjustment as often as needed, while continuing to edit the image in other ways. If you later decide you don't even need an adjustment, you can simply remove it!

The following adjustments are available:

- **Levels:** Adjust contrast and tonal range by shifting dark, light, and mid-tone values.

- **Curves:** Fine-tune lightness (luminance) values in the image or colour channel using a line graph.

- **Colour Balance:** Adjust colour and tonal balance for general colour correction in the image.

- **Brightness/Contrast:** Vary brightness and/or contrast.

- **Hue/Saturation/Lightness:** Vary hue, saturation, and/or lightness values.

- **Colourize**: Vary hue, saturation, and/or lightness to colourize an image.

- **Vibrance**: Boosts the saturation of low-saturation colours (while limiting saturation of already saturated colours).

- **Selective Colour:** Add or subtract a certain percentage of cyan, magenta, yellow, and/or black ink.

- **Channel Mixer:** Modify a colour channel using a mix of the current colour channels.

- **Gradient Map:** Remap greyscale (lightness) information in the image to a selected gradient.

- **Lens Filter**: Apply a colour filter to warm up (or cool down) your image.

- **Black & White Film**: Convert your colour image to black and white intelligently.

- **Threshold Filter:** Create a monochromatic (black and white) representation.

- **Posterize:** Apply the Posterize effect by limiting the number of lightness levels.

- **Negative Image:** Invert each colour, replacing it with an "opposite" value.

For more in-depth details on each adjustment, view the PhotoPlus help, click the Contents tab, and open the "Making Image Adjustments" book.

To create an adjustment layer:

1. From the Adjustments tab, select an adjustment. You can choose a default adjustment or a named preset by expanding the adjustment entry (click ▷).

2. In the Layers tab, the new adjustment layer is inserted above the active layer. The adjustment is applied to all underlying layers.

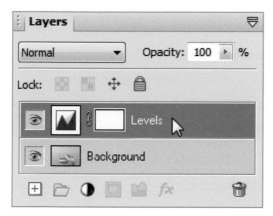

3. From the Adjustments tab, change the applied adjustment layer's settings to suit your requirements. For example, for a levels adjustment, you can drag the histogram pointers to alter levels.

Just like other layer types (Standard, Text, Shape, Filter, but not Background), adjustment layers can have a mask applied to them. By default, a mask thumbnail is shown on the adjustment layer. Select this to apply a mask to your adjustment layer. (See Using masks on p. 27.)

To save an adjustment layer as a new preset:

1. Select and then modify an adjustment layer in the Adjustments tab.

2. Click ⊞ **Add Preset**.

3. From the dialog, name your custom adjustment layer, and click **OK**.

Custom adjustments will appear under the adjustment's type in the tab's adjustment list.

To modify an adjustment layer:

1. Click the adjustment layer's name in the Layers tab.

2. From the Adjustments tab, modify the applied adjustment layer's settings.

To hide/show an adjustment layer:

• Click **Hide/Show Layer** on the Layers tab.

To delete an adjustment layer:

• (via Layers tab) Select the adjustment layer and click **Delete Layer**.
OR

• (via Adjustments tab) with the adjustment's settings pane showing, click **Delete Layer**. This removes the currently selected adjustment layer, so be careful not to remove additional adjustment layers in the Layers tab by clicking multiple times.

To reset an adjustment layer:

1. Click the adjustment layer's name in the Layers tab.

2. From the Adjustments tab, select **Restore Default Settings**.

To access layer properties for an adjustment layer:

• Right-click the layer name and choose **Properties**..

As with other layers, you can change the adjustment layer's name, set its opacity, blend mode, and/or blend ranges.

Clipping adjustment layers

Clipping allows you to restrict the scope of an **adjustment layer**, i.e. the adjustment influences **only** the layer immediately below it, rather than all underlying layers.

To clip an adjustment layer:

- Click 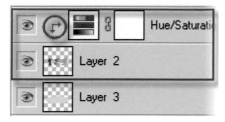 **Clip to Layer Below** on the selected adjustment layer (in the Adjustments tab).
  OR

  Right-click the adjustment in the Layers tab and select the same option.

You'll see your adjustment layer become indented, indicating that it is clipped to the layer below. The circled icon indicates a clipped layer.

To unclip a selected layer:

- In the Adjustments tab, click 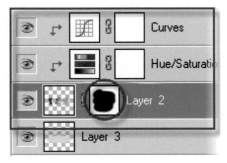 **Clip to Layer Below**.

One additional benefit of the clipping feature is that you can apply a mask to a lower layer (thumbnail circled below) so that adjustment layers above that are "clipped" to that lower layer. This saves you creating a mask per adjustment layer.

Retouching tools

The **Tools** toolbar includes an assortment of comparatively simple pressure-sensitive brush-based tools that come in handy at various stages of photo editing. Retouching tools work on Background and standard layers, but not on text layers or shape layers.

On the **Retouch Tools** flyout:

Red Eye Tool - for correcting the "red eye" phenomenon common in colour snapshots

Smudge Tool - for picking up colour from the click point and "pushing" it in the brush stroke direction

Blur Tool - for reducing contrast under the brush, softening edges without smearing colours

Sharpen Tool - for increasing contrast under the brush, enhancing apparent sharpness

Dodge Tool - for lightening an area

Burn Tool - for darkening an area

Sponge Tool - for increasing or decreasing the colour saturation under the brush

Replace Colour Tool - for swapping one colour for another

On the **Blemish Removal Tools** flyout:

Blemish Remover - for intelligently painting out skin blemishes

Scratch Remover - for filling in small gaps or dropouts in an image

Patch Tool - for painting out selected areas

Using PhotoFix

PhotoFix provides an image **adjustment** environment within PhotoPlus which simplifies the often complicated process of image correction. The studio environment offers the following key features:

- **Adjustment filters**
  Apply tonal, colour, lens, sharpening, and noise reduction filters.

- **Retouching filters**
  Apply red-eye correction, spot repair, straightening, and cropping.

- **Non-destructive operation**
  All filters are applied without affecting the original picture (by automatically creating a filter layer), and can be edited at any point in the future.

- **Powerful filter combinations**
  Create combinations of mixed adjustment filters for savable workflows.

- **Selective masking**
  Apply filters to selected regions using masks.

- **Save and manage favourites**
  Save filter combinations to a handy **Favourites tab**.

- **Viewing controls**
  Compare before-and-after previews, with tiled- and split-screen controls (horizontally and vertically). Use pan and zoom control for moving around your picture.

To launch PhotoFix:

- Click 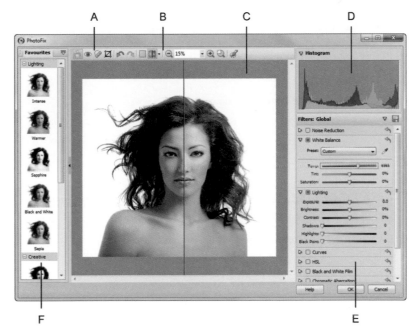 **PhotoFix** on the Photo Studio toolbar.

Let's get familiar with the PhotoFix interface showing a non-default **Split horizontal** view.

(A) Retouch tools, (B) Main toolbar, (C) Main Workspace,
(D) Histogram, (E) Filters, (F) Favourites.

Adjustments overview

Adjustments are made available to the right of the main window from the **Filters** section. Here's a quick overview of all the adjustments hosted in PhotoFix, some tool-based and some available as filters.

Retouch tools:

- **Red Eye**
  Removes the dreaded red eye effect from subject's eyes—commonly encountered with flash photography.

- **Spot Repair**
  Removes skin blemishes and other flaws.

- **Crop**
  Retains a print-size portion of your image while discarding the remainder. Great for home printing, then framing.

- **Straighten**
  Re-aligns slightly or wildly crooked photos by resetting the image's horizon, then applying an auto-crop.

These tools are supported by How To Help instructions within their dialogs.

Filter-based:

- **Noise Reduction**
  Use Luma and Chroma adjustments to reduce noise in photos taken in low light or from cameras with high ISO settings.

- **White Balance**
  "Cool down" or "warm up" your photo by adjusting lighting either by selecting presets or customizing temperature/tint combinations.

- **Lighting**
  Simple adjustments to a photo's exposure, brightness, contrast, shadows, and highlights.

- **Curves**
  Correct the tonal range of a photo, i.e. the shadow, midtone, and highlight regions—and control individual colour components.

- **HSL**
  Adjust the Hue, Saturation, and Lightness of your image independently.

- **Black and White Film**
  Intelligently apply greyscale by varying the grey tones of red, green or blue colours in your original image. Also apply colour tints.

- **Chromatic Aberration**
  Reduces red/cyan or blue/yellow fringing on object edges.

- **Lens Distortion**
  Fixes barrelling and pincushion distortion encountered when photographing straight-edged objects at close range.

- **Lens Vignette**
  Removes darkening in photo corners.

- **Unsharp Mask**
  Makes your image sharper at image edges—great for improving image quality after other adjustments have been made.

 Some adjustments can also be applied independently from the **Effects** menu.

To apply an adjustment (from a favourites preset):

1. From the **Favourites tab**, scroll the tab to review the categorized adjustments; select a preset or custom thumbnail.

2. Click **OK**.

When applied, your image layer is **automatically** converted to a non-destructive filter layer with a PhotoFix adjustment entry nested under the filter layer entry.

To apply an adjustment (using custom settings):

1. Review the available adjustments in the Filters section, before expanding the adjustment you want to apply by clicking ▷ **Expand filter.**

2. Modify the adjustment using sliders, check boxes, graph adjustments, and drop-down lists (you can also enter absolute values into available input boxes). The image will be adjusted automatically to reflect the new settings in the preview window.

   You'll notice the adjustment filter is enabled once a setting is changed, i.e. the ☐ **Enable/disable filter** option becomes greyed out (▣).

3. Click **OK**. A filter layer is created (as above).

To reset (and disable) a modified adjustment:

- Click ↰ **Reset settings** in the top-right corner of the adjustment's pane.

To edit PhotoFix adjustments:

- Double-click the PhotoFix entry on the filter layer. PhotoFix is launched with the previously set adjustments still applied.

Using PhotoFix masks

Masks in PhotoFix adopt the same principles as layer masks (see p. 27). In PhotoFix however, masking is used to apply adjustment filters to selected "painted" regions of your image or to protect painted regions from change. Painting is used exclusively to create PhotoFix masks.

Each new mask comprises the selected mask region, plus a set of adjustments applied to that mask. You can change the adjustments associated with the mask at a later date.

In the first example below, the model's hair has been masked by painting, allowing White Balance to be adjusted in that painted region only. Conversely, in the second example, the sky has been painted to protect it from masking, allowing light levels to be adjusted for Tower Bridge's stonework.

To achieve the above, PhotoFix uses two mask modes, namely **Mode Select** and **Mode Protect**. When you begin masking you'll need to decide which mode you want to use.

To apply a mask:

1. Select  **Create Mask** from the main toolbar.

2. In the Mask Brush pane, select the **Add Region** tool.

3. Adjust the settings to suit your requirements. For example, adjust Brush Size to paint larger or more intricate regions.

4. In the **Mode** drop-down list, choose one of the following options:

   • **Select**: Choose this if you want to apply the filter only to the regions you paint. This is the default setting.

   • **Protect**: Choose this if you want to apply the filter to all areas, except for those that you paint.

5. Using the brush cursor, paint the regions to be masked (selected areas are painted in green; protected areas in red).

6. Click **Accept**.

7. Apply your adjustments as described previously, which will make a change to your masked regions.

Adding multiple masks

So far we've looked at an individual mask applied to an image. However, PhotoFix also supports multiple masks where a different set of adjustments can be applied to each mask. You can therefore build up a patchwork of masked regions for absolute and selective control of image adjustments.

To apply additional masks:

1. In PhotoFix, click the down arrow on the Filters heading.

2. From the drop-down list, select **New**.

3. In the Mask Brush pane, change settings and paint as described previously in "To apply a mask".

4. Click **OK**. The new mask, named Mask 1, Mask 2, etc. is applied to your image.

5. Apply your adjustments as described previously.

6. Repeat the process for further masks.

Once applied, masks are applied cumulatively. The default global mask is applied to your image first, then Mask 1, then Mask 2, etc., if present. As a result, you may wish to rearrange the mask order for different results. You can also rename and delete masks.

To rearrange, rename or delete a mask:

1. From the down arrow on the Filters heading, select **Manage**.

2. From the dialog, select a mask and use appropriate supporting buttons.

3. Click **OK**.

To edit a mask:

1. From the down arrow on the Filters heading, select your mask name (a check indicates selection).

2. Modify your adjustments as described previously.

Saving favourites

If there's a specific filter setting (or combination of filters) you want to keep for future use it's easy to save it as a favourite. PhotoFix stores preset and custom favourites together in the Favourites tab. You can even create your own categories (e.g., MyAdjusts) within the tab for storing your custom adjustments.

To save a filter(s) as a new favourite:

1. Click [icon] **Save Filter** on the modified filter's pane.

2. From the dialog, enter a favourite name and pick a category to save the filter to. Optionally, click [...] to save to a new category.

If you want to further manage your favourites into user-defined categories, click **Manage Favourites** on the **Favourites tab's** ▽ **Tab Menu**.

5 Applying Image Effects

Overview: Applying special effects

Special effects are grouped into different categories, i.e. **distort**, **blur**, **sharpen**, **edge**, **noise**, **render**, **stylistic**, and **artistic**, which offer you a diverse choice of creative opportunities in PhotoPlus.

Before going ahead and applying your effects, it's a good idea to review Using filter layers (see p. 58) before deciding on your approach, i.e. whether you work non-destructively or destructively.

Each effect can be applied in one of several ways:

- on a filter layer, via an Effects dialog or via the Filter Gallery (non-destructive).

- on a standard layer, via an Effects dialog or via the Filter Gallery (destructive).

💡 Equally dramatic effects can be applied by using Warp tools on the Tools toolbar's flyout or 2D/3D layer effects via the Layers tab.

🖎 As with image adjustments (see Introduction to image adjustments on p. 35), you can use filter effects to improve the image, for example by sharpening, but more often the emphasis here is on the "creative" possibilities when effects are applied.

Using filter layers

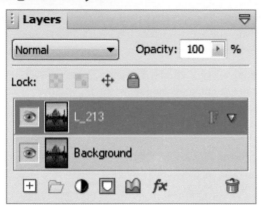

If you apply a filter effect to a standard or background layer, the layer is permanently altered. However, if you want the flexibility of being able to edit your filters at any point in the future (and don't want to destroy the layer contents) you can **convert** your standard or background layer to a **Filter Layer** (e.g., L_213).

Think of a Filter Layer as a way of keeping layer content independent of any filters you wish to use, with the flexibility of being able to manipulate a filter layer in the same way as other layers. Otherwise without filter layers, you would have to repeatedly undo your operations if you've had a rethink and no longer want to apply a specific filter.

When applied, filters are created within **filter groups**, nested individually under the Filter Layer. When you double-click a filter you display its specific settings. You can apply a blend mode and opacity to each filter, and additionally filter masking to the filter group.

 For added security, it's good practice to create a duplicate of any background layer you initially have.

To convert to a filter layer:

- In the Layers tab, right-click a standard or Background layer and choose **Convert to Filter Layer**.

    The layer now shows the letter "F" indicating that it is now a filter layer, and ready to have a filter applied.

To add filters to the filter layer:

1. Select the filter layer.

2. Add an adjustment via the **Image** menu (see p. 36).
    OR
    Add an effect via the **Effects** menu or via the Filter Gallery (see p. 64).

Each filter, as it is applied, is created within a filter group nested under the selected filter layer. In the example below, the Curves adjustment filter and Gaussian Blur effect filter is applied to the selected filter layer L_213. They'll be stored within Filter Group 1.

As a filter layer has all the properties of standard and Background layers, you may wish to review Introduction to layers (p. 19). Essentially, you can edit, hide/show, and delete filter layers as for standard layers, as well as apply a blend mode or opacity level.

To edit filter layer properties:

- In the Layers tab, right-click the filter layer and choose **Properties**.

Managing filter groups and specific filters

When you apply a filter to a filter layer it automatically creates a **filter group**. This allows you to store and manage a selection of filters more easily—you'll be able to control multiple filters in bulk by operating at the group level, e.g. to hide/show, delete, apply blend modes, and opacity to all filters simultaneously. Most operations can be applied equally to group or specific filter, except for masking, which can be used on filter groups but not on individual filters.

To hide/show a filter group/filter:

- Click the **Hide/Show Filter** button next to its name on the Layers tab.

  OR

  Right-click the filter and select **Disable Filter** (or **Enable Filter**).

  OR

  Right-click the filter group and select **Disable Filter Group** (or **Enable Filter Group**).

To delete a filter group/filter:

- Right-click the filter (or filter group) and select **Delete Filter (Group)**.

To create an empty filter group:

Right-click a filter layer and select **Add Filter Group** from the flyout menu.

Just as layers can adopt different blend mode and opacity levels the same is true of filter groups and individual filters. For a refresh on these concepts, see Using blend modes and Adjusting opacity/transparency on p. 31 and p. 25, respectively.

You can use the Blend Options dialog to make blend mode and opacity changes with a dynamic preview, updating as you make change.

To apply a blend mode:

1. Right-click the filter group (or filter) and select **Blend Options**.

2. From the dialog, select an option from the **Blend Mode** drop-down list.

3. Click **OK**.

To change opacity:

- From the above dialog, enter an **Opacity** level.

Editing filters

The core objective of filter layers is to host filters applied to your image. Once a filter is applied, it's likely that you may want to edit it at a later date.

To edit a filter:

1. Double-click the filter entry, e.g. Gaussian Blur.
   OR
   Right-click the filter and select **Edit Filter**.

2. The filter can then be edited via dialog or Filter Gallery. Adjust the filter and click **OK**.

Using filter masks

In an identical way to layer masks (see p. 27) you can apply a **mask** to a filter layer. However, masks can additionally be used for selective filter control for image correction or artistic reasons. These are called **filter masks**, which limit the influence of any applied filter(s) to that masked region only. Filter masks are applied either automatically (from a selection existing before applying a filter) or manually (after you've applied the filter) to a **filter group** (but never to an individual filter).

See Using masks (see p. 27) for more details on masking and masking controls.

To create a filter mask (from a selection):

1. Make a selection on which your mask will be based, e.g. a brush selection around the subject of interest. By default the area outside the selection is masked (i.e. not affected by the filter), while the selection area retains the applied filter. If you want to do the opposite, choose Invert from the **Select** menu.

2. In the Layers tab, select the filter layer to which you wish to apply a filter.

3. Add an adjustment via the **Image** menu.
    OR
    Add an effect via the **Effects** menu or via the Filter Gallery.

    The filter is created within an automatically created filter group, which applies a mask automatically.

4. (Optional) Fine-tune the filter by double-clicking the filter entry and editing the settings.

To create a filter mask (by mask painting):

1. With no selections present, in the Layers tab, select the filter layer to which you wish to apply a filter.

2. Add an adjustment via the **Image** menu.
    OR
    Add an effect via the **Effects** menu or via the Filter Gallery.

3. Right-click the created filter group and select **Add Mask** from the flyout menu and then one of the following from the submenu:

    - **Reveal All** for a transparent mask

    - **Hide All** for an opaque mask.

    A mask thumbnail appears to the left of the filter name.

4. Paint or draw on your image using a suitable greyscale value set as your foreground colour. The mask thumbnail updates accordingly.

The mask thumbnail would apply a mask which produces a vignette effect. As you can also paint with different greyscale levels you can achieve even more complex masking effects.

To disable (enable) a mask:

- Right-click the filter group and select **Disable Mask** (or **Enable Mask**) from the flyout menu.

To delete a mask:

- Right-click the filter group and select **Delete Mask** from the flyout menu.

Using the Filter Gallery

The Filter Gallery offers a one-stop studio environment for applying **single** or **multiple** filter effects. The gallery hosts sets of filter thumbnails which are categorized into different effect categories (e.g., Distort, Blur, Sharpen, Edge, Artistic, Noise, Render, etc.). Thumbnails are shown in expandable categories.

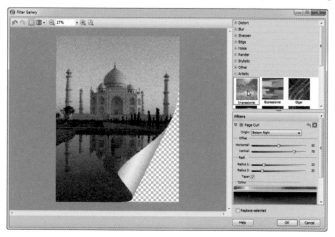

The Filter Gallery offers the following key features:

- Application of individual or multiple filter effects simultaneously.

- Preview window with zoom and pan support.

- Optional **Before** and **After** views arranged as tiles or split-screen, both horizontally and vertically.

You can apply filters via the Filter Gallery in one of two ways:

- permanently to a standard layer.
  OR
  on a Filter Layer (see p. 58), allowing you to protect your image layer, as well as manage your filters at a later date.

To view the Filter Gallery:

- Click 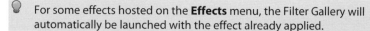 **Filter Gallery** on the Photo Studio toolbar.

> For some effects hosted on the **Effects** menu, the Filter Gallery will automatically be launched with the effect already applied.

To add a filter in the Filter Gallery:

1. Expand your chosen effect category by clicking the ⊞ **Expand** button (click ⊟ to collapse).

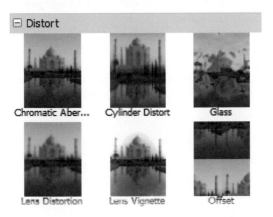

Click on an effect thumbnail to apply it to your image.

The applied filter is shown in a **Filters** stack in the lower-right corner of the Filter Gallery. The properties of any selected effect will be displayed in the expanded area under the effect name—you can alter and experiment with these at any time. The filter shows on a light background to indicate selection.

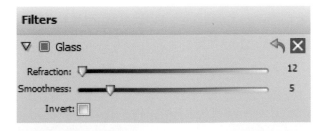

Use the **Undo** button to undo recent changes to the filter (or the **Redo** button to re-apply the changes).

2. Adjust sliders (or enter input values) until your filter suits your requirements. Some filters offer check boxes, drop-down lists, and additional controls (e.g., Advanced settings). The large preview window updates automatically as you adjust any values.

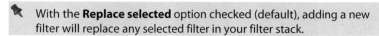

With the **Replace selected** option checked (default), adding a new filter will replace any selected filter in your filter stack.

To add multiple filters:

- Uncheck **Replace selected**, then add one or more additional effects as described above.

Any filter can be temporarily disabled, reset, or deleted once applied.

To disable: Click ▣, then click ☐ to enable again.

To reset: Click ↩. Any changes to settings are reverted back to the filter's defaults.

To delete: Click ✕. The filter is removed from the stack.

The effect's properties are expanded by default but can be collapsed to make more of the Filters stack visible.

To collapse/expand filter properties:

- To collapse, click the ▽ button preceding the filter effect name. To expand again, click the ▷ button.

To replace a filter:

1. Ensure **Replace selected** is checked.

2. Select the filter you wish to replace by clicking anywhere in the filter's pane. On selection, the selected filter shows a lighter background, e.g, Gaussian below.

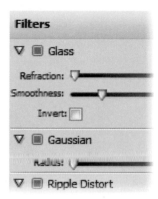

3. Select a replacement filter from an effect category. Your selected filter is replaced in the stack with no change made to the existing stack order.

The order in which effects appear in the effect list may produce very different results. If you're not happy with the current order, PhotoPlus lets you drag and drop your effects into any position in the stack. Effects are applied in the same way that layers are applied, i.e. the most recently added filter always appears at the bottom of the list and is applied to the picture last (after the other filters above it).

Filters can be moved around the filter list to change the order in which they are applied to the photo.

To reorder filters:

*   Drag and drop your filter into any position in the stack. A dotted line indicates the new position in which the entry will be placed on mouse release.

Applying 2D layer effects

Layer effects can be applied to the contents of standard layers, text layers, or shape layers. Standard or "2D" layer effects like shadow, glow, bevel, and emboss are particularly well adapted to text, while 3D layer effects (covered elsewhere; p. 70) create the impression of a textured surface.

Unlike image adjustments and **Effects** menu manipulations, layer effects don't directly change image pixels—they work like mathematical "lenses" that transform how a layer's bitmap appears. Since the settings are independent, you can adjust them ad infinitum until you get the result you want!

Here's an example of each effect applied to the letter "A".

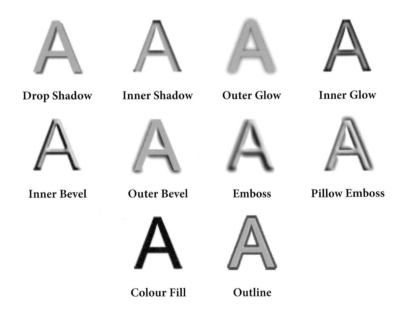

Drop Shadow	Inner Shadow	Outer Glow	Inner Glow
Inner Bevel	Outer Bevel	Emboss	Pillow Emboss
	Colour Fill	Outline	

- **Drop Shadow** adds a diffused shadow "behind" solid regions on a layer.

- **Inner Shadow** adds a diffused shadow inside the edge of an object.

- **Outer Glow** adds a colour border outside the edge of an object.

- **Inner Glow** adds a colour border inside the edge of an object.

- Bevel and Emboss/**Inner Bevel** adds a rounded-edge effect inside an object.

- Bevel and Emboss/**Outer Bevel** adds a rounded-edge effect (resembling a drop shadow) outside an object.

- Bevel and Emboss/**Emboss** adds a convex rounded edge and shadow effect to an object.

- Bevel and Emboss/**Pillow Emboss** adds a concave rounded edge and shadow effect to an object.

- **Colour Fill** lets you apply a specific colour to a layer.

- **Outline** applies a border effect to the edge of an object. See Creating outlines in PhotoPlus Help.

To apply a shadow, glow, bevel, or emboss effect:

1. From the Layers tab, select a layer and click *fx* **Add Layer Effects**.

2. In the dialog, apply an effect by checking its check box in the list at left. You can apply multiple effects to the layer.

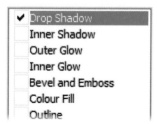

3. To adjust the properties of a specific effect, select its name and adjust the dialog controls. Adjust the sliders, drop-down list, or enter specific values to vary each effect. Options differ from one effect to another.

4. Click **OK** to apply the effect or **Cancel** to abandon changes.

Applying 3D layer effects

3D layer effects are just as easy to apply, but they're a bit more complex than their 2D cousins (see p. 68). Actually, there's an easy way to get started with them: simply display the **Instant Effects tab** and preview its gallery thumbnails.

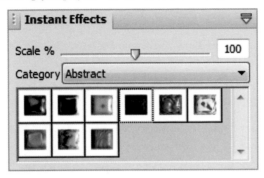

In the tab you'll see a variety of remarkable 3D surface and texture presets grouped into wide-ranging "themed" categories (e.g., Glass Text, Abstract, Wood, Metal). Click any thumbnail to apply it to the active layer. Assuming the layer has some colour on it to start with, you'll see an instant result!

> 💡 If hidden, make this tab visible via **Window>Studio Tabs**.

To apply an Instant Effect to the active layer:

- From the **Instant Effects** tab, select a category, then click a gallery thumbnail.

- To make the effect appear smaller or larger in relation to the image, drag the **Scale** slider or type a value in the tab.

You can apply an effect from the Instant Effects tab, edit it (using the Layer Effects dialog) and then save it as a custom preset in a user-defined category (you'll have to create and select the category first). To save the preset, right-click in the tab and choose **Add Item**. From the dialog, you can adjust the Scale of the effect and have your thumbnail preview stored as a Rectangle or as Text (using the letter "A"). For either type, the thumbnail will appear in the gallery.

fx If you want to have complete flexibility when creating 3D effects, you can click the **Add Layer Effects** button on the Layers tab.. The dialog is shared for both 2D and 3D effects—simply check the 3D Effects box and experiment with the settings (enable other 3D check boxes as appropriate).

For more information about creating 3D filter effects, see PhotoPlus Help.

3D effects overview

✔ 3D Effects
    3D Bump Map
        Function
            Advanced
    2D Bump Map
✔ 3D Pattern Map
        Function
            Advanced
    2D Pattern Map
    Reflection Map
    Transparency
✔ 3D Lighting

Suppose you've applied a 3D layer effect preset from the Instant Effects tab, and then you bring up the Layer Effects dialog. On inspecting the settings used in the preset, the first thing you'll notice is that several boxes may be checked.

- **3D Effects** is a master switch for this group, and its settings of **Blur** and **Depth** make a great difference; you can click the "+" button to unlink them for independent adjustment.

- **3D Pattern Map** allows for blend mode, opacity, depth, displacement and softening adjustments, along with a choice of gradient fills. This is checked depending on the type of instant effect selected.

- **3D Lighting** provides a "light source" without which any depth information in the effect wouldn't be visible. The lighting settings let you illuminate your 3D landscape and vary its reflective properties.

To apply 3D Effects:

- Click *fx* **Add Layer Effects** on the Layers tab and check **3D Effects** in the Layer Effects dialog. Adjust the "master control" sliders here to vary the overall properties of any individual 3D effects you select.

  - **Blur** specifies the amount of smoothing applied. Larger blur sizes give the impression of broader, more gradual changes in height.

  - **Depth** specifies how steep the changes in depth appear.

  - The ⊞ button is normally down, which links the two sliders so that sharp changes in Depth are smoothed out by the Blur parameter. To adjust the sliders independently, click the button so it's up (not blue).

- Check a 3D effect in the **3D Effects** list which reflects the 3D effect you can achieve. Procedures for each are detailed below.

3D Reflection Map

The **3D Reflection Map** effect is used to simulate mirrored surfaces by selection of a pattern (i.e., a bitmap which possesses a shiny surface) which "wraps around" a selected object. Patterns which simulate various realistic indoor and outdoor environments can be adopted, with optional use of 3D lighting to further reflect off object edges. The effect is often used in combination with the Transparency option.

Transparency

The uniform transparency of a layer and its objects (with 3D layer effects applied) can be controlled via the Layers tab with the Opacity option (see rear heart shape in example below). However, for more sophisticated transparency control, transparency settings can instead be set within the Layer Effects dialog. The effect can be used to create more realistic transparency by independently controlling transparency on reflective (edges) and non-reflective (flat) areas of the object (see front heart shape below).

 Use this effect in conjunction with reflection maps and multiple directional light sources for ultra-realistic glass effects.

3D Lighting + Layer
Opacity 50%

3D Lighting +
Transparency effect

Warp tool effects

The **Warp Tools** from the Tools toolbar's **Warp Tools** flyout work as a group and act as brush-on effects rather than dialog-based filters. Most of the tools shift pixels as the brush passes over, while the **Unwarp** brush undoes the effects of the other tools. The actual amount of pixel displacement depends on the direction or amount of brush movement, the brush tip, and the tool's settings, selectable from the brush context toolbar.

Merging bracketed photos

High Dynamic Range (HDR) merge, or tone mapping, is used to combine bracketed photos or scanned images from film, each shot taken at different exposure levels (typically one each for highlights, midtones, and shadows) and within seconds apart. Your camera can't capture all exposure levels in a single shot, so by bringing together multiple photos you can expand your image's dynamic range which would otherwise be impossible in a single shot.

Typically, scenes of high contrast such as landscapes, sunsets or indoor environments (with strong lighting) are suited to HDR Merge.

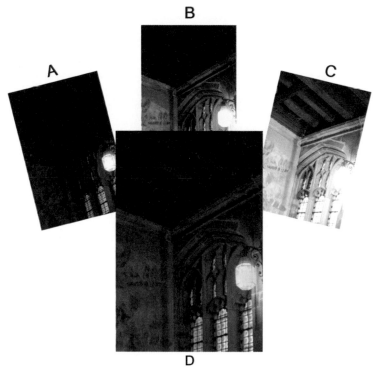

*(**A**)Exposure for Highlights, (**B**) Midtones,*
*(**C**) Shadows, (**D**) and the Merged output.*

For good results, it's important to bear the following points in mind:

- Many modern cameras offer **auto-bracketing** which automatically takes several shots at different exposure levels. A two-EV spacing is considered to be optimum for most occasions. Alternatively, shoot with manual exposure set.

- Always shoot the same scene! Your output is based on a composite of the same scene.

- Take as many shots as is needed to cover your required dynamic range.

- Use a tripod for optimum camera stability. Also avoid photographing objects affected by windy conditions (e.g., moving tree branches).

- Ensure **Aperture priority** is set on your camera (see your camera's operating manual for more details).

The HDR merge is a two-stage process, firstly to select the source files (JPG or raw) for merging, and then performing the merge itself after having adjusted merge settings to optimize the output. The process can be carried out directly on source files without loading them into your project in advance.

PhotoPlus lets you optionally save the merged HDR image to one of several formats (namely OpenEXR, HDR and HD Photo), which can be opened at a later date, saving you from having to align and merge your original images again.

To select and merge bracketed photos:

1. From the Startup Wizard, click **HDR Photo Merge.**
   OR
   Select **HDR Merge** from the **File** menu.

2. From the **HDR Source Files** dialog, click **Add**.

3. Browse to, then select multiple files from the chosen folder—use **Ctrl**-click or **Shift**-click for selecting non-adjacent or adjacent images. Click **Open**. The files listed show image name and an exposure value equivalent to your camera's exposure setting (the values are not just for show—they're crucial for successful HDR merging).

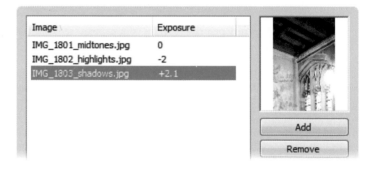

Click the **Add** button to add more photos or the **Remove** button to exclude a selected photo.

For scanned images (from camera film) which won't possess EXIF-derived Exposure values, you can click the **Edit Exposure** button to add your own exposure values to entries if you've kept a record (or you could just add +2.0, 0, and -2 then experiment with the results).

4. (Optional) Uncheck **Align images** if you're sure your source images are perfectly aligned (perhaps by a third-party application). Otherwise, PhotoPlus will automatically attempt to align each photo's corresponding pixel data.

5. (Optional) Check **Infer film response curve** to affect a tone curve needed to accurately process scanned images (from camera film). Otherwise, keep unchecked for digital camera use.

6. Click **OK**. The Merge HDR dialog is displayed, showing a preview of your intermediate HDR image.

> ★ Don't worry if your initial results look less than desirable. You're only half way towards your stunning image but you'll need to modify the HDR image using a series of adjustments next.

To adjust your intermediate image:

1. From the **HDR Merge** dialog, an image preview is displayed, along with a merge file list and merge settings. Optionally, uncheck an image from the upper-right list to exclude it from the merge.

2. Drag the **Compression** slider to a new value—use your eye to judge the best merge results, but also the supporting Histogram to ensure that the tonal range fits into the visible graph without clipping. The option compresses or expands the dynamic range by dragging right or left, respectively.

3. Set a **Brightness** level to make the image either lighter or darker.

4. Adjust the **Black Point** slider right to shift the histogram's left-most edge making all affected pixels in the shadow region turn black.

5. Reduce **Local Contrast Radius** to alleviate image "flatness" when compressing the dynamic range (see Compression above).

6. Set the **Temperature** to give a warmer "reddish" or cooler "blueish" look; drag to the right or left, respectively.

7. Adjust the **Saturation** value to reduce or boost the colour in your image.

8. Check **Output 16-bits per channel** if you're looking for the highest level of detail in your merged output.

9. Click **OK**.

10. From the next dialog, you'll be asked if you want to save the intermediate HDR Image or just continue as an untitled project.

- Click **Yes** to preserve the HDR image. This saves having to select, align, and merge images again, but you'll still need to reapply any adjustments previously made. Select a file location, file format, name for your file, then click **Save**. The file format, OpenEXR (.exr), Radiance (.hdr), or HD Photo (.hdp), can be chosen from the drop-down list.
  OR

- Click **No** if you don't need to preserve the HDR image (you'll have to select, align, and merge again). Your merge results will be the basis for an Untitled project.

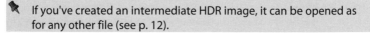

If you've created an intermediate HDR image, it can be opened as for any other file (see p. 12).

6 Manipulating Images

Making a selection

In any photo editing program, the **selection tools and techniques** are as significant as any of the basic brush tools or commands. The basic principle is simple: quite often you'll want to perform an operation on just a portion of the image. To do this you must define an active selection area.

The wide range of selection options in PhotoPlus lets you:

- Define just about any selection shape, using various drawing and painting techniques.

- Modify the extent or properties of the selection (see p. 89)

- Carry out various manipulations on the selected pixels, including cut, copy, paste, rotate, adjust colours, apply special effects, etc. (see p. 94)

Selection basics

Although the techniques for using the various selection methods differ, the end result is always the same: a portion of the active layer has been "roped off" from the rest of the image. The boundary is visible as a broken line or **marquee** around the selected region (see above).

Whenever there's a selection, certain tools and commands operate **only** on the pixels inside the selection—as opposed to a condition where nothing is selected, in which case those functions generally affect the entire active layer.

 You may occasionally (especially if the marquee is hidden) find yourself using a tool or command that seems to have no effect... it's probably because there's still a selection somewhere, and you're trying to work outside the selection. In this case, just cancel the selection.

To cancel the selection (select nothing):

- From the **Select** menu, click **Deselect**.

The opposite of selecting nothing is selecting everything...

To select the entire active layer:

- Choose **Select All** from the **Select** menu.

For partial selection of opaque pixels, you can **Ctrl**-click the layer thumbnail (in Layers tab).

> If your image has multiple layers, and you switch to another layer, the selection doesn't stay on the previous layer—it follows you to the new active layer. This makes sense when you realize that the selection doesn't actually include image content—like an outline map, it just describes a region with boundaries.

Selection tool options

PhotoPlus offers a very wide range of other selection methods, and a variety of commands for modifying the extent or properties of the selected pixels—all available from the Tools toolbar. Note that the selection tools work on Background and standard layers, but not on text layers or shape layers.

Available from:	Tools
Selection Tools flyout	**Rectangle Selection Tool**—drag out a rectangular selection area of your chosen size (use the **Ctrl** key to constrain to a Square area).
	Ellipse Selection Tool—drag out an ellipse selection area (use **Ctrl** key to constrain to a circle).
	QuickShape Selection Tools flyout—provides different variable shapes, including pie, star, arrow, heart, spiral, wave, and so on. The shapes can be further "morphed" into other custom QuickShapes by dragging node handles around the QuickShape.

Lasso Tools flyout

Freehand Selection Tool—lets you draw a freehand (irregular) line which is closed automatically to create an irregularly shaped selection area.

Polygon Selection Tool—lets you draw a series of straight-line segments (double-click to close the polygon).

Magnetic Selection Tool—lets you trace around an object edge creating a selection line that snaps to the edge as you drag.

directly from toolbar

Magic Wand Tool—lets you select a region based on the colour similarity of adjacent pixels—simply click a starting pixel then set a **Tolerance** from the context toolbar. It works much like the fill tool, but the result is a selected region rather than a region flooded with a colour.

Smart Selection Brush—lets you create your selection as a series of brush strokes.

from the **Select** menu

Paint to Select mode—lets you use standard painting or editing tools as selection tools.

Text Tools flyout

Text Selection Tool—lets you create a selection in the form of text. Click with the tool to display the Text cursor. Type your text, format as needed, and click **OK**. (See Creating and editing text on p. 150.)

For any selection tool, the context toolbar includes combination buttons (**New***, **Add**, **Subtract**, and **Intersect***) that determine the effect of each new selection operation. For example, starting with a square selection (created with the **New** button), here's what a second partly overlaid square (shown with a solid line) might produce with each setting:

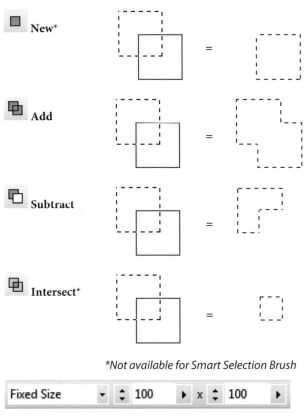

*Not available for Smart Selection Brush

For Rectangle and Ellipse Selection tools, the context toolbar additionally lets you set a **Fixed Size** or **Fixed Aspect**, or number of Rows or Columns (Rectangle Selection Tool only) in advance of creating your selection—great if you have a clear idea of the selection area required!

Selecting layer opacity/transparency

New layers are transparent (they have an alpha channel) , but once you've placed pixels on the layer you'll be able to select between the layer's pixels (i.e., their opacity) and remaining transparency.

To create a selection from a layer's opacity/transparency:

- For selection of **Opacity**:

  In the Layers tab, **Ctrl**-click on the layer's image thumbnail.

- For selection of **Transparency**:

  As above, but additionally select **Invert** from the **Select** menu.

Colour Range

As an intelligent colour selection method, i.e. where selection is based on "tagging" a specific range of colours or tones in the image, choose **Colour Range** from the **Select** menu.

To select a colour range:

1. Choose **Colour Range** from the **Select** menu. The Colour Range dialog opens with a selection preview window.

2. To make an initial selection:

    *   To tag a particular colour or tone group, such as "Reds" or "Midtones," choose the group's name from the **Select** drop-down list.
        OR

        Click **Colour Picker** to sample a chosen pixel colour from the image in your workspace. With this method, the **Tolerance** slider lets you include a wider or narrower range of colours in the selection, based on the chosen colour.

 Once you've made an initial selection, you can use the **Add Colour** and **Subtract Colour** buttons to include/exclude further colours in the selection by single-click or by dragging across the image to tag/untag a colour range. Alternatively, for initial selection, drag across the image to select ranges.

> 💡 With **Add/Subtract Colour** tools initially selected, you can also drag across a section of the image.

Meanwhile, the dialog provides visual feedback.

1. If **Show Selection** is checked, the greyscale preview selection window shows tagged values as brighter, with untagged pixels darker. To customize what's displayed in the workspace, choose an option from the Preview list: "None" shows the original image, "White Matte" shows tagged pixels through a white background, and so on.

2. Click **OK** to confirm the selection, or **Cancel** to abandon changes.

> 📌 🔄 **Restore default settings** reverts back to original dialog settings.

Storing selections

You can **store selections** (i.e., just the marqueed region and per-pixel selectedness data) as part of either the current image or any open image file, and **load** a stored selection at any time. It's often useful to be able to "grab" the same region of an image at different phases of working on it. And, for repetitive tasks (preparing web buttons, for example) on different but graphically similar files, by storing a selection you can reuse it rather than having to recreate it for each file.

Selections are created and stored exclusively as alpha channels in the Channels tab; Once stored, they can be retrieved from the tab at any time.

As each alpha channel behaves like a mask (p. 27) you can paint on the alpha channel at different greyscale levels for different levels of "selectedness". The White or light portions of the mask reveal layer pixels (make them more opaque). Black or dark portions hide layer pixels (making them more transparent).

To store a selection:

1. Make a selection on your image.

2. In the Channels tab, select  **Create Channel From Selection**. The channel appears with a default name (rename via double-click if needed).

Use ⊞ **New Channel** on the Channels tab to create an empty channel on which you can design (e.g., paint) in greyscale for different levels of "selectedness".

To load a selection:

- In the Channels tab, select **Create Selection From Channel**.

To delete a stored selection:

- In the Channels tab, select **Delete Channel**.

Modifying a selection

Once you've used a selection tool to select a region on the active layer, you can carry out a number of additional steps to fine-tune the selection before you actually apply an effect or manipulation to the selected pixels.

Transforming the selection

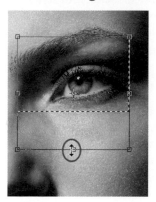

The **Selection Deform Tool** on the **Tools** toolbar's **Deform Tools** flyout lets you transform, scale or rotate any already drawn selection area. With the tool enabled, square nodes on the mid-points and corners of any selected area can be dragged (opposite).

Look for the cursor changing between resize and rotate modes when hovering over a node.

Use in conjunction with the **Ctrl** key to transform the selection area without constraint, creating a **skewed transform** (drag nodes as appropriate). The **Alt** key resizes the area about its centre, while the **Shift** key maintains the area's aspect ratio. It's also possible to move the small centre of rotation "handle" in the centre of the transform to produce an arc rotational movement rather than rotating around the area's centre (by default).

> Holding down the **Shift** key whilst rotating will cause a movement in 15 degree intervals.

Making the selection larger or smaller

If the selection you've made isn't quite the right shape, or doesn't quite include all the necessary pixels (or perhaps includes a few too many), you can continue to use the selection tools to add to, or subtract from, the selected region.

To add or subtract to/from the existing selection with a selection tool:

- Select the tool and drag while holding down the **Shift** or **Alt** key, respectively. The newly selected pixels don't have to adjoin the current selection—it's possible to select two or more separate regions on the active layer.

Modifying the selection

Once you've made a selection, several modify selection operations can be used in combination to alter the selection area. Feather, smooth, contract, and expand operations are possible from a single **Modify Selection** dialog, along with the popular Grow, Similar, and Invert available separately. Combining the operations in a dialog improves efficiency, and lets you preview your modified selection **directly on the image** as you make changes. Several preview methods are possible.

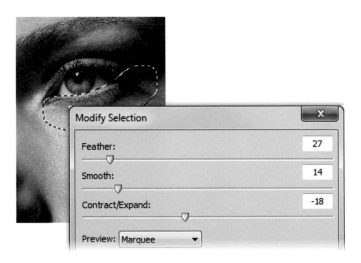

To modify a current selection:

1. From any Selection context toolbar, select **Modify Selection**.

2. From the **Modify Selection** dialog, you can enter a specific pixel value for the type of operation you require.

   • **Feather**: Use to apply feathering to the edge of an existing selection (but before applying any editing changes). Enter the width (in pixels) of the transition area. A higher value produces a wider, more gradual fade-out. See Soft-edged and hard-edged selections on p. 93.

   • **Smooth**: If the selected region has ragged edges or discontinuous regions (for example, if you've just used the Magic Wand Tool), use the option to control the extent of smoothing.

   • **Contract/Expand**: Move the slider left to contract (shrink) the borders of the selection, or right to extend its borders.

3. Select a preview method from the **Preview** drop-down list—choose to preview as an Overlay, in Greyscale, or use different Mattes.

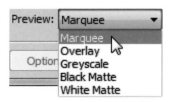

The **Modify** item on the **Select** menu (or right-click on selection) provides a submenu with the above options, along with other intelligent selection options:

- **Grow** and **Similar** both expand the selection by seeking out pixels close (in colour terms) to those in the current selection. **Grow** only adds pixels adjacent to the current selection, while **Similar** extends the selection to any similar pixels in the active layer.

  Both options use the tolerance setting entered for the Magic Wand Tool on the context toolbar. As the tolerance increases, a larger region is selected. Typically when using these tools, you'll start by selecting a very small region (the particular colour you want to "find" in the rest of the image).

- Choose **Border** to create a new selection as a "frame" of a specified pixel width around the current selection.

- The **Invert** option selects the portion of the active layer outside the current selection. Unselected pixels become selected, and vice versa.

Soft-edged and hard-edged selections

Anti-aliasing and **feathering** are different ways of controlling what happens at the edges of a selection. Both produce softer edges that result in smoother blending of elements that are being combined in the image. You can control either option for the Standard and QuickShape Selection tools, using the **Feather** input box (or slider) and **Anti-alias** check box on the context toolbar.

- **Anti-aliasing** produces visibly smooth edges by making the selection's edge pixels semi-transparent. (As a layer option, it's not available on the Background layer, which doesn't support transparency.)

- If an anti-aliased selection (for example, one pasted from another image) includes partially opaque white or black edge pixels, you can use **Matting** options on the **Layers** menu to remove these pixels from the edge region, yielding a smoother blend between the selection and the image content below. (Fully opaque edge pixels are not affected.)

- **Feathering** reduces the sharpness of a selection's edges, not by varying transparency, but by *partially selecting* edge pixels. If you lay down paint on a feathered selection, the paint will actually be less intense around the edges.

- **Threshold** converts a feathered, soft-edged selection into a hard-edged selection (use **Select>Modify>Threshold**). As with feathering, you won't see an immediate effect on the image, but painting and other editing operations will work differently inside the selection.

Manipulating a selection

Moving the selection marquee

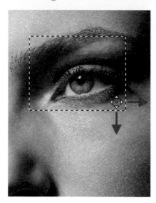

  Sometimes, you need to adjust the position of the marquee without affecting the underlying pixels. Any time you're using one of the selection tools, the cursor over a selected region changes to the **Move Marquee** cursor, which lets you drag the marquee outline to reposition it.

> ✦ You're only moving the selection outline—not the image content inside it.
>
> 💡 You can also use the keyboard arrows to "nudge" the selection marquee.

Once you have selected your chosen pixels, the operations which can be performed include moving, cutting, copying, duplicating, pasting and deleting. You use the **Move Tool** to drag the selection *plus* its image content. (See Modifying a selection on p. 89).

Using the Move Tool

The  **Move Tool** is for pushing actual pixels around. With it, you can drag the content of a selection from one place to another, rather than just moving the selection outline. To use it, simply click on the selection and drag to the new location. The selected part of the image moves also.

- If nothing is selected, dragging with the Move Tool moves the entire active layer. (Or, if the Move Tool's **Automatically select layer** property is selected on its context toolbar, the tool moves the first visible item's layer beneath the move cursor when you click to move.)

- When the Move Tool is chosen, you can also use the keyboard arrows to "nudge" the selection or active layer.

- The "hole" left behind when the image content is moved exposes the current background colour (on the Background layer), or transparency (see above; on standard layers), shown with a "checkerboard" pattern.

- To duplicate the contents of the selection on the active layer, press the **Alt** key and click, then drag with the Move Tool.

- As a shortcut if you're working with any one of the selection tools, you can press the **Ctrl** key to switch temporarily to the Move Tool. Press **Ctrl+Alt** to duplicate. Release the key(s) to revert to the selection tool.

Cut/Copy/Delete/Paste

Cut and copy operations on selections involving the Clipboard work just as in other Windows programs.

- To copy pixels in the selected region, press **Ctrl+C** or click the **Copy** button on the **Standard** toolbar. (You can also choose **Copy** from the **Edit** menu.)

- To cut the selected pixels, press **Ctrl+X** or choose **Cut** from the **Edit** menu.

- To delete the selected pixels, press the **Delete** key or choose **Clear** from the **Edit** menu.

> Cut or deleted pixels expose the current background colour (on the Background layer) or transparency (on standard layers). If you want to create transparency on the Background layer, first "promote" it to a standard layer by right-clicking its name on the Layers tab and choosing **Promote to Layer**.

- If nothing is selected, a cut or copy operation affects the whole active layer, as if **Select All** were in effect.

When pasting from the Clipboard, PhotoPlus offers several options.

- To paste as a new image in an untitled window, press **Ctrl+V** or click the **Paste as New image** button on the **Standard** toolbar. (Or select from the **Edit>Paste** menu.)

- To paste as a new layer above the active layer, press **Ctrl+L** or choose **Paste>As New Layer** from the **Edit** menu.

- To paste into the current selection, press **Shift+Ctrl+L** or choose **Paste> Into Selection** from the **Edit** menu. The Clipboard contents appear centred in the currently selected region. (This choice is greyed out if there's no selection, or if the active layer is a text layer.) This option is useful if you're pasting from one layer to another. Because the selection marquee "follows" you to the new layer, you can use it to keep the pasted contents in registration with the previous layer.

- To duplicate part of the active layer on the same layer, press the **Alt** key and click, then drag with the Move Tool. (Or if you're working with a selection tool, press **Ctrl+Alt** and drag to duplicate.)

Changing image and canvas size

You probably know that image dimensions are given in **pixels** ("dots of paint" that comprise a screen image). In PhotoPlus there are options to change the **image size** and to change the **canvas size**, but what's the difference and how do you perform each resize?

Changing image size

Changing the image size means scaling the whole image (or just a selected region) up or down. Resizing is actually a kind of distortion because the image content is being stretched or squashed.

You will change the image size when:

- enlarging the image for print.

- reducing the image for on-screen display.

- reducing the image to create a thumbnail for a website.

The Image Size dialog lets you specify a new size for the whole image, in terms of its screen dimensions and/or printed dimensions.

To resize the image for on-screen display:

1. Choose **Image Size** from the **Image** menu.

2. Select the **Resize layers** option to link the Pixel Size (screen) settings to the Print Size or Resolution settings.

3. To retain the current image proportions, check **Maintain aspect ratio**. Uncheck the box to alter the dimensions independently.

4. Select a preferred scale (either "Pixels" or "Percent") in the drop-down list.

5. Select a resampling method. As a rule, use **Nearest Pixel** for hard-edge images, **Bilinear Interpolation** when shrinking photos, **Bicubic Interpolation** when enlarging photos, and **Lanczos3 Window** when best quality results are expected.

6. Enter new **Width**, **Height** or **Resolution** values.

7. Click **OK**.

To resize the image for print:

1. Choose **Image Size** from the **Image** menu.

2. Uncheck **Resize layers**.

3. To retain the current image proportions, check **Maintain aspect ratio**. Uncheck the box to alter the dimensions independently.

4. Select your preferred units of measurement and resolution. The pixel size will automatically alter with print size adjustment.

5. Click **OK**.

Changing canvas size

Changing the canvas size just involves adding or taking away pixels around the edges of the image. It's like adding to the neutral border around a mounted photo, or taking a pair of scissors and cropping the photo to a smaller size. In either case, the remaining image pixels are undisturbed so there's no distortion.

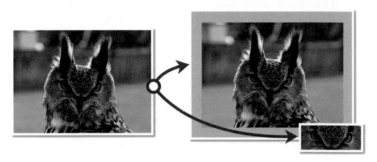

You will change the canvas size when:

- you want to add a border to your image (without changing the size of the image itself).

- you crop an image.

There are several ways of changing the image's native canvas size. You can use the Crop Tool (see Cropping an image on p. 104) or the Crop to Selection (p. 108) command. For more accurate canvas resizing (both enlargements or reductions), the Canvas Size dialog that lets you specify where pixels should be added or subtracted.

To change canvas size:

1. Choose **Canvas Size** from the **Image** menu.

2. Enter **New Width** and/or **New Height** values (the current values are also shown for comparison). Alternatively, select the **Relative** check box to enter the number of units you want to add to the existing width and height values—for example, 5 pixels, 1 cm, 100 points, 10 percent, and so on.

3. In the Anchor box, click to position the image thumbnail with respect to edges where pixels should be added or subtracted. For example, if you want to extend the canvas from all sides of the image, click the centre anchor point.

4. Click **OK**.

 If the canvas size is increased, the new canvas area is filled (on the Background layer) with the current background colour and (on standard layers) with transparency.

Straightening photos

As an image adjustment, the **Straighten Tool** can be used to align a crooked image back to horizontal (e.g., restoring proper horizontal alignment in a scanned image that wasn't aligned correctly on the scanner). Use the tool to trace a new horizon against a line in the image—the image automatically orients itself to the drawn horizon.

Before
(horizon line drawn by dragging)

After

You can straighten using one of two methods: As a separate tool used directly on your image (next page) (destructive) or via the PhotoFix (non-destructive) studio environment (see p. 46).

To straighten (via Straighten Tool):

1.   ⬜ ▾ 🖫 On the **Tools** Toolbar, expand the **Crop Tools** flyout and click the **Straighten Tool**.

2.   On the context toolbar, choose an option from the **Canvas** drop-down list. This lets you decide how your straightened image will be displayed:

   - **Crop** - Crops and adjusts the straightened image so that it displays on the largest possible canvas size, without displaying any border.

   - **Expand to Fit** - Increases the canvas size to display the entire straightened image. The border area is filled with the current background colour.

   - **Original Size** - Displays the straightened image within the original canvas dimensions. The border area is filled with the current background colour.

   ♀ On the image that needs straightening, look for a straight line on the image to which you can set the new horizon (e.g., the divide between the land and sea above).

3.   (Optional) Uncheck **Rotate All Layers** to restrict the operation to the active layer only. Otherwise all layers are rotated.

4.   Using the Straighten cursor, drag a horizon from one end of the image's line to the other (the length of the horizon is not important) then release. The image orients itself to the new line.

Cropping an image

Cropping is the electronic equivalent of taking a pair of scissors to a photograph, except of course with a pair of scissors there is no second chance! Cropping deletes all of the pixels outside the crop selection area, and then resizes the image canvas so that only the area inside the crop selection remains. Use it to focus on an area of interest—either for practical reasons or to improve photo composition.

 For more on why you may wish to crop, or for inspiration, see Importance of cropping in PhotoPlus Help.

 You can crop larger areas when photos are shot at a high resolution. Keep this in mind before taking photos and make sure your camera is set to its highest resolution and image quality.

Using the Crop Tool

Before

After
(Rectangular Crop)

PhotoPlus allows you to crop unconstrained, or to a standard or custom print size.

To crop unconstrained:

1. 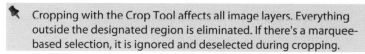 From the Tools toolbar's **Crop Tools** flyout, select the **Crop Tool**. Ensure the **Unconstrained** option is set in the context toolbar's first drop-down list.

2. Drag out a rectangle to create an unconstrained rectangle, then fine-tune the areas dimensions if needed by dragging the edges.

> You can constrain the crop area to a square, by holding down the **Ctrl** key while dragging.

3. To crop to the designated size, double-click inside the crop area.

The **Shading** check box and **Opacity** option on the context toolbar sets the shade colour and transparency of the unwanted region outside the rectangle, respectively. Uncheck **Shading** to view only the rectangle, with no shading and full transparency.

> Cropping with the Crop Tool affects all image layers. Everything outside the designated region is eliminated. If there's a marquee-based selection, it is ignored and deselected during cropping.

To crop to a specific print size or resolution:

1. Select the 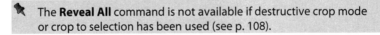 **Crop Tool** from the Tools toolbar.

2. Then either:

    - For print sizes, choose a **pre-defined** print size (expressed in inches or centimetres) from the first drop-down list in the context toolbar. Both portrait and landscape crop regions can be selected—e.g., 4 x 6 in for portrait, 6 x 4 in for landscape).
    OR

    - If you need to set a **custom** size, enter values into the Height and Width drop-down lists, choosing inches or centimetres as measurement units in advance—note that the print size changes to "Custom" after entering new values. The Print Size resolution alters automatically while honouring your print Width and Height.

3. Drag out your crop area to create your constrained rectangle or square (if Custom).

4. Double-click the crop area to crop to the designated size.

By default, the Crop Tool in PhotoPlus is "non-destructive", as the context toolbar's **Destructive** option is unchecked. This means that at any point, you can remove or adjust the original crop applied to a photo (provided the project was saved as an SPP—see Saving a file on p. 15).

For information on destructive, permanent cropping, see p. 108.

To undo a non-destructive crop:

- From the **Image** menu, click **Reveal All**.

> The **Reveal All** command is not available if destructive crop mode or crop to selection has been used (see p. 108).

Using rule of thirds

Use the **Thirds grid** check box on the context toolbar for improving photo composition. A 3 x 3 rectangular grid with equally spaced lines (two vertically, two horizontally) is superimposed on top of your photo when the check box is selected.

Moving and resizing the grid allows the main subject of your photo to be offset and balanced against a foreground or background feature within the photo.

Position a main item of interest in the photo where any two lines intersect within the crop grid (four intersections are possible). This is known as the "rule of thirds" which will help you find the most balanced composition where your eyes are drawn to the main subject (for more information, see Rule of Thirds in PhotoPlus Help).

Double-click to crop the photo to the outer grid dimensions.

Destructive (or permanent) cropping

Destructive (or permanent) cropping can be applied to any image by selecting the **Destructive** option on the Crop Tool's context toolbar before applying the crop.

 Applying a permanent crop to your photo will reduce the file size of your project.

 Cropping in destructive mode permanently discards the pixels outside of the crop area. If your opened photo is cropped and you then click Save, it will be permanently altered. It's recommended to save a copy of your photo first and apply the crop to the copy.

Cropping to a selection

You can also crop an image to any **selection area**, no matter what shape, as defined with one of the selection tools.

If the Rectangle or Ellipse Selection Tool is used, you can make your selection a Fixed Size, defined in pixels, from the tool's context toolbar. This crop to pixel operation is heavily used when creating precisely dimensioned web graphics or specific ebook cover dimensions.

Alternatively you can crop to shape (above) by using one of a range of shaped selections using the QuickShape Selection Tool.

To crop the image to the selection:

- Choose **Crop to Selection** from the **Image** menu.

If the selection region is non-rectangular, the left-over surrounding region will be either transparent (on a standard layer) or the current background colour (e.g., white).

 Cropping to the selection affects all image layers. Everything outside the selected region is eliminated.

Flipping and rotating

Flipping and rotating are standard manipulations that you can carry out on the whole image, the active layer, a path, or just on a selection. Flips are used to change the direction of a subject's gaze, fix composition, and so on, whereas rotation is an orientation tool for general purpose use.

Flip Horizontal

Flip Vertical

Rotate
15° anti-clockwise

Rotate
10° clockwise

To flip:

- Choose either **Flip Horizontally** or **Flip Vertically** from the **Image** menu, then select **Image**, **Layer**, **Selection** or **Path** from the submenu.

To rotate:

1. Choose **Rotate** from the **Image** menu.

2. From the flyout menu, select an option based on the object (Image, Layer, or Selection), rotation angle (90° or 180°), and the direction (Clockwise or Anti-clockwise) required.

3. You can also select **Custom**, to display a **Rotate** dialog, from which you can do all of the above but instead set your own custom angle, even down to fractional degrees.

Deforming

The [icon] **Deform Tool** (Tools toolbar) lets you move, scale, rotate, or skew a selection or layer. Start by making a selection if desired, then choose the Deform Tool. For either selection or layer, a rectangle appears with handles at its corners and edges, and a fixed point (initially in the centre of the region). If there's no selection, the rectangle includes the whole active layer.

For example, a layer can be deformed using scale and skew operations.

Scale down layer contents from top-right corner of rectangle; revealing the background colour.

Skew from top-right corner handle by dragging with the Ctrl key pressed.

The layer contents are skewed for artistic effect.

Mesh warping

The **Mesh Warp Tool** (Tools toolbar) works like the Deform Tool outfitted with complex curves. It lets you define a flexible grid of **nodes** and **lines** that you can drag to distort an image, or part of an image (or layer). You can edit the mesh to vary its curvature, and even custom-design a mesh to match a particular image's geometry—for example, curves that follow facial contours—for more precise control of the warp effect.

> The Mesh Warp Tool works on Background and standard layers, but not on text layers or shape layers.

When you first select the tool, a simple rectangular mesh appears over the image, with nine nodes: one at each corner, one at the centre, and one at the midpoint of each edge. Straight lines connect adjacent nodes. A context toolbar also appears to support the Mesh Warp Tool.

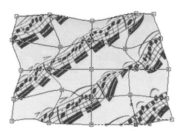

The straight line segments are actually bendable curves. When you alter the contours of the mesh and distort the initial rectangular grid, the underlying image deforms accordingly. To change the mesh, you simply move nodes, node attractor handles, or connecting lines; add or subtract nodes as needed; and/or edit nodes to change the curvature of adjoining lines.

To hide the mesh for a better preview of the image:

- Click the ⊞ **Hide/Show Mesh** button on the Mesh context toolbar. Click again to reveal the mesh for editing.

The **Deform Mesh** option makes it easy to move, scale, skew, or rotate a mesh **region** about a fixed point; a region is the area enclosed by multiple nodes. It works just like the standard Deform Tool (described on p. 110) but on multiple nodes instead of individual ones.

To deform the mesh systematically:

1. **Shift**-click or drag a marquee to select multiple nodes.

2. Click the 🖉 **Deform Mesh** button on the Mesh Warp Tool's context toolbar. A selection rectangle appears around the designated nodes (you may need to zoom in to see this), with a fixed point in the centre and handles at its corners, sides, and centre.

   - To deform the mesh region, drag from any corner or midpoint handle.

   - To rotate the mesh region, drag from just outside any corner handle.

   - To move the fixed point, move the cursor over the fixed point symbol until the cursor changes, then drag (this then lets you perform arc rotations). To move the entire region, drag from elsewhere within the region.

   - Watch the Hintline for details on many key-assisted options such as skew, squash/stretch, and perspective effects. In this respect, the tool works almost exactly like the regular Deform Tool (see p. 110).

3. Click the button again to return to standard mesh warping.

Using Cutout Studio

Cutout Studio offers a powerful integrated solution for cutting out part of an image on an active Background or standard layer. In doing so, you can separate subjects of interest from their backgrounds, either by retaining the subject of interest (usually people, objects, etc.) or removing a simple uniform background (e.g., sky, studio backdrop). In both instances, the resulting "cutout" creates an eye-catching look for your image, and lets you present cutouts layer-by-layer— great for simulating subject/background combinations and artistic collages.

The latter background removal method is illustrated in the following multi-image example.

> 🖎 A checkerboard on the second image's background upon preview is used to indicate areas to be discarded.
>
> 🖎 Cutout Studio works on Background and standard layers, but not on text layers or shape layers.

To launch Cutout Studio:

1. Select an image to be cut out.

2. Select ![icon] **Cutout Studio** from the Photo Studio toolbar.

    OR

    Select **Cutout Studio** from the **Edit** menu.

Cutout Studio is launched.

Selecting areas to keep or discard

A pair of brushes for keeping and discarding is used to "paint" areas on your active layer. The tools are called **Keep Brush** and **Discard Brush**, and are either used independently or, more typically, in combination with each other. When using either tool, the brush paints an area contained by an outline which is considered to be retained or discarded (depending on brush type). A configurable number of pixels adjacent to the outline area are blended.

To select areas for keeping/discarding:

1. In Cutout Studio, click either 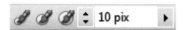 **Keep Brush Tool** or **Discard Brush Tool** from the left of the Studio workspace.

2. (Optional) Pick a **Brush size** suitable for the area to be worked on.

3. (Optional) Set a **Grow tolerance** value to automatically expand the selected area under the cursor (by detecting colours similar to those within the current selection). The greater the value the more the selected area will grow.

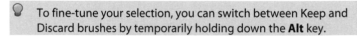

4. Using the circular cursor, click and drag across the area to be retained or discarded (depending on Keep or Discard Brush Tool selection). It's OK to repeatedly click and drag until your selection area is made.

   The 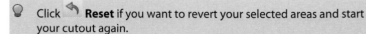 **Undo** button reverts to the last made selection.

> To fine-tune your selection, you can switch between Keep and Discard brushes by temporarily holding down the **Alt** key.

5. Click **OK** to create your cutout.

You'll now see your active layer with the selected areas cut away (made transparent).

> Click **Reset** if you want to revert your selected areas and start your cutout again.

Changing output settings

You can set the level of transparency and pixel blending at the cutout edge by adjusting the **Width** output settings. Control of the cutout edge lets you blend your cutout into new backgrounds more realistically.

To change output settings:

1. Drag the **Width** slider to set the extent (in pixels) to which "alpha" blending is applied inside the cutout edge. This creates an offset region within which blending occurs.

2. Adjust the **Blur** slider to apply a level of smoothing to the region created by the above Width setting.

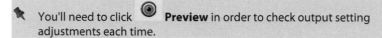 You'll need to click **Preview** in order to check output setting adjustments each time.

Refining your cutout area

Erase and Restore touch-up tools can be used to refine the cutout area within the studio before completing your cutout.

The touch-up tools are brush based and are only to be used to fine-tune your almost complete cutout—use your Keep and Discard brush tools for the bulk of your work!

To restore or remove portions of your cutout:

1. With your cutout areas already defined, click 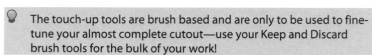 **Preview** (Output settings tab). You can use the button to check your cutout as you progress.

2. Click the 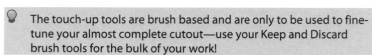 **Restore Touch-up Tool** or 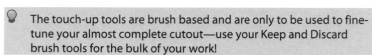 **Erase Touch-up Tool** button from the left of the Studio workspace.

3. Paint the areas for restoring or erasing as you would with the brush tools.

If you've touched up part of your image between each preview, you'll be asked if you want to save or discard changes.

7 **Colour and Greyscale**

Colour modes

PhotoPlus operates in several colour modes to let you work in standard and higher levels of colour or tonal detail—these are 8-bits/channel RGB (or 8-bits/channel Greyscale) and the more detailed 16-bits/channel RGB (or 16-bits/channel Greyscale). Editing in 8 bits/channel mode will use 256 levels per colour channel, as opposed to 16-bits/channel, which uses 65,536 levels per channel.

As a rule of thumb, use 16-bit working for "as-your-eyes-see-it" image accuracy.

If you work with 16-bit images, you'll probably want to benefit from the optimum colour or tonal information throughout your project.

PhotoPlus also lets you **manually** choose modes:

	Choose..	Then pick.
when creating a new image	**New Image** (Startup Wizard) or **File>New from Startup Wizard.** or **File>New**	Colour Mode: RGB or Greyscale Bit Depth: 8 or 16 bits per channel
at any time	**Image>Colour Mode**	RGB 8 Bits/Channel RGB 16 Bits/Channel Greyscale 8 Bits/Channel Greyscale 16 Bits/Channel
importing raw images	from the **Bit Depth** drop-down list (**Output Format** section)	8 Bits/Channel 16 Bits/Channel
when outputting the results of an HDR Merge	**File>HDR Merge.**	Output 16-bits per channel

If you no longer need to work at a high level of detail (16 Bits/channel), you can convert your image to 8-bit mode which results in smaller file sizes and allows you to take advantage of PhotoPlus's range of special filter effects.

To switch from 16-bits/channel to 8-bits/channel working:

- From the **Image** menu, select **Colour Mode**, and pick an 8-bits/channel option from the submenu.

 To check which mode is currently set, the Title bar shows the mode after the file name, e.g. CRW_4832.CRW @ 20%, 3088 x 2056, **RGB 16 Bits/Channel**.

Choosing colours

Foreground and background colours

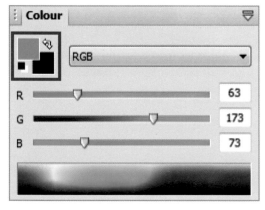

At any given time, PhotoPlus allows you to work with just two colours—a **foreground** colour and a **background** colour. These are always visible as two swatches on the Colour tab indicated opposite.

The foreground colour is set to green (RGB 63:173:73) and the background colour to black.

The Colour tab makes it possible to set the working colour model before colour selection: **RGB** (Red, Green, Blue); **CMYK** (Cyan, Magenta, Yellow, Black) ; **HSB** sliders (Hue, Saturation, Brightness); **HSL** sliders (Hue, Saturation, Lightness); **HSL Colour Wheel**; **HSL Colour Box**; or **Greyscale**.

To set the mode:

- Choose an option from the RGB ▼
  drop-down list.

Defining colours

Now, a few things to remember about how these colours are used:

- When you draw a selection, shape, or use the paintbrush tools, you could apply the foreground colour.

- However, the black text in the design could be created after swapping foreground and background colours using the tab's 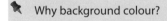 button. Loading the foreground and background colour with two frequently used colours is a great way to boost productivity when painting and drawing.

> 📌 Why background colour?
>
> When you cut, delete, or erase an area on the Background layer, the area exposes the currently set background colour—as if that colour were there "behind" the portion of the image being removed. (Layers other than the Background layers behave differently: on these, a removed area exposes transparency.)

To define foreground and background colour:

1. Select the  **Colour Pickup Tool** on the Tools toolbar.

    As you move the cursor around your photo, a swatch appears displaying the colour under the cursor.

    R:239 G:146 B:0 O:255

2. (Optional) On the context toolbar, set the **Sample Size** (pickup region) as a single "Point Sample", "3 x 3 Average" or "5 x 5 Average" area. The last two options lets you sample an "averaged" colour over a square pixel region, ideal for sampling halftone images, i.e. when point sampling is not suitable.

3. Left-click with the tool anywhere on an image to "pick up" the colour at that point as the new foreground colour. Right-click to define a new background colour.

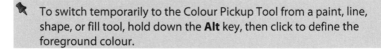

To switch temporarily to the Colour Pickup Tool from a paint, line, shape, or fill tool, hold down the **Alt** key, then click to define the foreground colour.

OR

1. On the Colour tab, click and move the mouse pointer (dropper cursor) around the **Colour Spectrum**. As you move the dropper cursor around the spectrum, the tab's active colour swatch updates to the colour at the cursor position.

2. Left-click in the spectrum to set a new foreground colour, and right-click to set a new background colour.

OR

- On the Colour tab, use the slider(s) or enter numeric values in the boxes to define a specific colour. The selected swatch updates instantly.

To swap foreground and background colours, click the ⇅ double arrow button next to the swatches. To reset the colours to black and white, click the ■ black and white mini-swatch at the bottom left of the swatch.

Storing colours

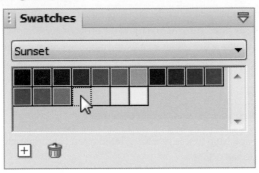

If you want to save colours that you want to work with frequently, you can store them in the Swatches tab as thumbnails (this avoids continually defining colours in the Colour tab). The Swatches tab hosts galleries of categorized colour thumbnails.

> 💡 If hidden, make this tab visible via **Window>Studio Tabs**.

You can store your currently selected foreground colour (in Colour tab) to the currently selected category (e.g., Sunset); you can also create categories yourself into which you can add your own thumbnails. The Swatches tab also lets you choose pre-defined colours from a range of "themed" categories (e.g., Earth, Fruits, Pastel, and web browser safe).

To add a colour to the Swatches tab:

1. From the Swatches tab, pick the correct category to store the colour.

2. Click the ⊞ **New Swatch** button to add the Colour tab's foreground colour to the current gallery.

To apply a colour from the Swatches tab:

*   Click to select any gallery thumbnail—the Colour tab's foreground colour will update ready for use in painting, drawing, filling, etc.

8 Painting, Drawing and Text

Painting and brushes

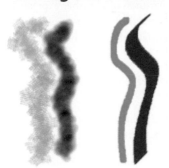

 The **Paintbrush Tool** and **Pencil Tool** on the Tools toolbar are the basic tools for painting and drawing freehand lines on the active layer. They work on Background and standard layers, but not on text layers or shape layers. The tools work by changing pixels on the layer.

The **Paintbrush Tool** applies **anti-aliasing** to its brush strokes to ensure brush edges appear very smooth irrespective of the brush's Hardness setting. In contrast, the **Pencil Tool** (used just like the Paintbrush Tool) always creates a hard-edged line.

The **Brush Tip tab** hosts a comprehensive collection of brush presets grouped into various categories; each category can be switched to via a drop-down list and displays a gallery. Note that each sample clearly shows the brush tip and stroke; the number indicates the brush diameter. The brush tip determines the thickness and many other properties of the painted line.

> 💡 You can also create your own brush from within the tab.

If you scroll down the gallery, you'll note that some brushes have hard edges, while others appear fuzzy, with soft edges. The hardness of a brush is expressed as a percentage of its full diameter. If less than 100%, the brush has a soft edge region within which the opacity of applied colour falls off gradually.

Brush attributes (blend mode, opacity, size, and flow) can be modified via a context toolbar (along with more advanced Brush Options) and, if necessary, saved for future use with the Tool Presets tab.

If a more bespoke brush tip is required, you can also customize your own brush tip and save it in its own user-defined category. (See Creating your own brush tips in PhotoPlus Help for details.)

An important factor when applying brush strokes is the level of opacity applied to the brush. This attribute affects brush strokes significantly when the stroke is applied onto already transparent standard layers. The greater the opacity the more opaque the brush stroke. Experiment to achieve the right combination of opacity and colour for your brush strokes.

To use the Paintbrush or Pencil tool:

1.   From the **Tools** toolbar's **Brush Tools** flyout, select the **Paintbrush Tool** or **Pencil Tool**.

2.   Choose a brush tip preset on the **Brush Tip** tab. If you've picked a Basic brush, set a brush colour (i.e. the foreground colour) from the Colour tab before painting.

3.   (Optional) Change brush tip's attributes, if necessary, on the context toolbar. These changes do not affect the brush presets present in the Brush Tip tab.

4.   Drag the cursor on the active layer, holding the left mouse button down to paint in the foreground colour.

Brush options

The Brush Options dialog, accessible from the context toolbar's **Brush** option, lets you customize a brush or define properties for a new one. As you vary the settings, you can see the effect of each change in the preview window.

Painting using pen tablets

Brush strokes can be applied directly to the page by using your mouse or, if available, a pen tablet; the latter method is ideally suited for applying pressure-sensitive strokes to your project. PhotoPlus supports pressure sensitivity, with tablet calibration and key assignment possible directly from within the program (via Pressure Studio).

Stamping and spraying pictures

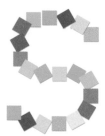

The **Picture Brush Tool** works like a custom brush that sprays a series of pre-defined or custom images at regular intervals as you drag. Used in conjunction with the Brush Tip tab you can select from a variety of picture brushes in different categories, and you can import Paint Shop Pro "picture tubes".

You can use the tool either to "stamp" single images at specific points or lay out a continuous stream of repeating pictures as in the letter "S" on the left.

The Picture Brush tool works on Background and standard layers, but not on text layers or shape layers.

To draw with the Picture Brush:

1. From the **Tools** toolbar's **Brush Tools** flyout, select the **Picture Brush Tool.**

2. On the Brush Tip tab, pick a brush tip from one of the categories.

   To control image elements, right-click a brush from any Brush Tip tab category, and choose **Brush Options**.

3. From the context toolbar, set the opacity and size of the image elements produced by using the **Opacity** and **Diameter** option. For pen tablet users, check stylus **Size** and/or **Opacity** to make these brush properties respond to your pressure device.

4. To "stamp" single images at specific points, click in various places on your canvas. To spray a continuous line of images, drag a path across the page.

If you right-click on any gallery sample, you can manage categories, and access brush options.

Creating custom picture brushes

Each picture brush has its own stored **master image** with image elements arranged in rows and columns. To define a picture brush, you first create a new master image and then choose **New Brush** via right-click in a user-defined category in the Brush Tip tab. (For details, see PhotoPlus Help.)

Erasing

Sometimes the rubber end of the pencil can be just as important to an artist as the pointed one. The Eraser Tools flyout on the Tools toolbar provides ways of enhancing an image by "painting" with transparency rather than with colour.

Use the **Standard Eraser** for replacing colours in an image either with the background colour or with transparency (on Background or other standard layers, respectively).

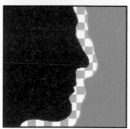

Use the **Background Eraser** for erasing pixels similar to a sampled reference colour underlying the cursor crosshair—great for painting out unwanted background colours.

Use the **Flood Eraser** for filling a region with transparency, erasing pixels similar to the colour under the cursor when you first click.

In general, you can set tool properties for each tool including brush characteristics, opacity, tolerance, flow, and choose a brush tip. The Eraser tools work on Background and standard layers, but not on text layers or shape layers.

To erase with the Standard Eraser:

1. Select **Standard Eraser** from the **Tools** toolbar's **Eraser Tools** flyout.

2. (Optional) Change attributes, especially brush **Size** and **Opacity**, on the context toolbar.

   For erasing with an airbrush effect or hard-edged brush, check the **Airbrush** or **Hard Edge** option.
   For tablet users, pressure sensitivity can be switched on via Brush Options (click **Brush** thumbnail); ensure the **Controller** drop-down list is set to "Pressure" on selected attributes.

3. Drag with the tool on the active layer. On the Background layer, erased pixels expose the current background colour. On other layers, they expose transparency.

To erase with the Background Eraser:

1. Select **Background Eraser** from the **Tools** toolbar's **Eraser Tools** flyout.

2. (Optional) Change properties on the context toolbar:

   - For tablet users, pressure sensitivity can be switched on via Brush Options (click **Brush** thumbnail); ensure the **Controller** drop-down list is set to "Pressure" on selected attributes.

   - The **Tolerance** setting determines the breadth of the colour range to be erased.

   - With "Contiguous" limits (the default), the tool erases only within-tolerance pixels **adjacent** to each other and within the brushes width; this tends to restrict erasure to one side of an edge or line. When you set "Discontiguous" limits, all matching pixels are erased under the brush even if they are non-adjacent (great for removing uniform background like sky). The "Edge Detected" setting can improve erasure along one side of a contrasting edge or line.

Contiguous   *Discontiguous*

- With "Continual" sampling (the default), the reference colour is repeatedly updated as you move the cursor. Sampling "Once" means erasure is based on the colour under the crosshair when you first click. Use the "Background Swatch" setting to use the current background colour (Colour tab) as the reference.

- You also have the option of protecting the current foreground colour from erasure (**Protect foreground**).

3. Drag with the tool on the active layer to erase pixels similar to a sampled reference colour directly under the brush tip.

 If you use the tool on the Background layer, it's promoted to a standard layer.

To erase with the Flood Eraser:

1. Select **Flood Eraser** from the **Tools** toolbar's **Eraser Tools** flyout.

2. (Optional) Change properties on the context toolbar.

3. Click (or click and drag) with the tool on the active layer to erase pixels close in colour (based on the Tolerance range) to the colour under the cursor when you first click. If you use the tool on the Background layer, it's promoted to a standard layer.

Erasing using pen tablets

For tablet users, PhotoPlus supports pressure sensitivity, with tablet calibration and key assignment possible directly from within the program (via Pressure Studio).

Using patterns

The  **Pattern Tool** (Tools toolbar's **Clone Tools** flyout) lets you paint a pattern directly onto your canvas. In effect, it "clones" any pattern bitmap you've selected while providing the flexibility to paint wherever you wish, and control opacity, blend mode, and so on. Like the Clone Tool, the Pattern brush picks up pixels from a source—in this case, the bitmap pattern—and deposits them where you're drawing. You can choose a pre-defined, tiled bitmap pattern from the Patterns dialog, or define your own patterns.

As an example, patterns can be used effectively as a painted background, perhaps when creating web graphics.

Filling a region

Filling regions or layers is an alternative to brushing on colours or patterns. Making a selection prior to applying a fill, and setting appropriate options, can spell the difference between a humdrum effect and a spectacular one.

The **Fill Tools** flyout on the Tools toolbar includes two tools for filling regions with colour and/or transparency: **Flood Fill** and **Gradient Fill**. In addition, you can use the **Edit>Fill** command to apply either a **colour** or **pattern** fill. As with paint tools, if there is a selection, the Fill tools only affect pixels within the selected region. If you're operating on a shape or text layer, the **Gradient Fill** tool can be used to adjust the interior of the object(s) on the layer.

Flood and pattern fills

The **Flood Fill Tool** works on Background and standard layers, replacing an existing colour region with the foreground colour. How large a region is "flooded" with the fill colour depends on the difference between the colour of the pixel you initially click and the colour of surrounding pixels.

To use the Flood Fill Tool:

1. Select the **Flood Fill Tool** from the **Tools** toolbar's **Fill Tools** flyout.

2. Set tolerance and layer fill options on the context toolbar.

    *   A pattern can be applied as a fill from the context toolbar by picking a **Pattern** (click the thumbnail) from the gallery, then choosing the **Fill** drop down list to be "Pattern".

3. Click with the tool where you want to start the fill.

The **Edit>Fill** command lets you flood-fill a region on a standard layer using any colour, not just the foreground colour. On the other hand, it's strictly a solid colour flood without the subtleties of the Flood Fill Tool's properties. Simply choose the command to display the Fill dialog.

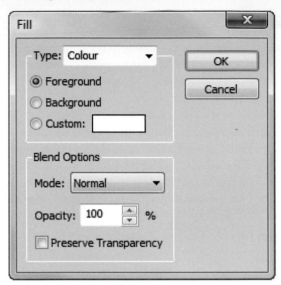

To use the Fill command:

- Choose **Fill** from the **Edit** menu. The Fill dialog appears.

- For a flood fill, set the **Type** to Colour.

- Choose whether the fill colour is to be the current **Foreground** colour, **Background** colour or a **Custom** colour.

- Specify the blend mode and opacity of the fill.
  If you check **Preserve Transparency**, transparent areas will resist the flood colour; otherwise, everything in the selection or layer will be equally washed with the fill.

- For a Pattern fill, set the **Type** to **Pattern**.
  The blend options are the same, but in this mode instead of choosing a colour you can fill a region with any pattern stored in the Patterns dialog. Click the pattern sample to bring up the gallery of pattern thumbnails (see Using patterns on p. 134 for more information).

Gradient Fill Tool

Whereas solid fills use a single colour, all gradient fills in PhotoPlus utilize at least two "key" colours, with a spread of hues in between each key colour, creating a "spectrum" effect. You can fine-tune the actual spread of colour between pairs of key colours. Likewise, a gradient fill in PhotoPlus can have either **solid transparency**—one level of opacity, like 50% or 100%, across its entire range—or **variable transparency**, with at least two "key" opacity levels and a spread of values in between. (Remember that opacity is simply an inverse way of expressing transparency.)

The ⬜ **Gradient Fill Tool** lets you apply variable colour and/or transparency fills directly to a layer.

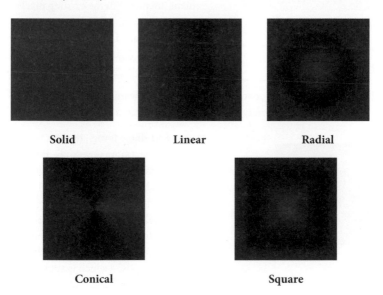

Solid   **Linear**   **Radial**

Conical   **Square**

Applying a gradient fill on any kind of layer entails selecting one of the fill types, editing the fill colours and/or transparency in a Gradient dialog, then applying the fill. However, gradient fills behave differently depending on the kind of layer you're working on.

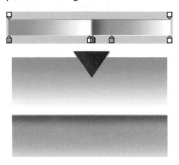

On **standard and Background layers**, the tool creates a "spectrum" effect, filling the active layer or selection with colours spreading between the key colours in the selected gradient fill. The fill is applied rather like a coat of spray paint over existing pixels on the layer; colour and transparency properties in the fill gradient interact with the existing pixels to produce new values. In other words, once you've applied the fill, you can't go back and edit it (except by undoing it and trying again).

Transparency works in a comparable way, affecting how much the paint you apply is "thinned." At full opacity, the fill completely obscures pixels underneath.

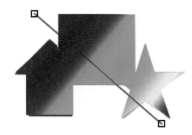

On **text and shape layers**, the Gradient Fill Tool is even more powerful—the fill's colour and transparency properties remain editable. Technically, the fill is a property of the layer, and the shape(s) act as a "window" enabling you to see the fill. Thus a single fill applies to all the shapes on a particular layer—note the gradient fill opposite which is applied across three QuickShapes present on the same layer.

Transparency gradients determine which portions of the object you can see through. Note that the Flood Fill Tool doesn't work with text or shapes. When first drawn, a shape takes a Solid fill using the foreground colour. You can change the fill type as described below.

To apply a gradient fill:

1. Select 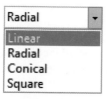 **Gradient Fill Tool** from the **Tools** toolbar's **Fill Tools** flyout.

2. Select a fill type from the context toolbar. Choose Linear, Radial, Conical or Square.

Radial	▾
Linear	
Radial	
Conical	
Square	

3. To choose a preset or to edit the fill's colours and/or transparency values, click the colour sample on the context toolbar.

    The Gradient dialog appears, where you can select a preset fill from the default or a pre-defined gallery (select a category e.g., Blues, Greens, from the drop-down list).

    Click ▽ to access further options such as adding, editing or deleting categories and adding and deleting custom fills. See PhotoPlus Help for details on how to edit gradient fills.

4. (Optional) Check **Reverse** to swap the direction of your chosen fill.

5. (Optional) Uncheck **Transparency** if you don't want transparency (if present) in your chosen gradient fill to be preserved; otherwise, the fill's transparency is maintained when the fill is applied.

6. Once you've defined the fill, click with the tool where you want to start the fill and drag to the point where you want it to end.

To change a text or shape layer's fill type, or edit its colour(s):

- Double-click the text/shape layer (or right-click and choose **Edit Fill**). OR

- Choose the **Gradient Fill Tool** and use the context toolbar.

Either option lets you choose a fill type, and/or click the colour (or gradient) sample to edit the fill.

On text or shape layers, the **fill path** (the line in the illustration above) remains visible even after you've applied the fill, and you can adjust the fill's placement after the fact by dragging the fill path's end nodes with the Gradient Fill Tool.

Cloning a region

The ☁ **Clone Tool** is like two magic brushes locked together. While you trace or "pick up" an original drawing with one brush, the other draws ("puts down") an exact duplicate somewhere else—even in another image.

When retouching, for example, you can remove an unwanted object from an image by extending another area of the image over it (note the pickup area is positioned over the sea rather than the original boat).

The tool acts on the active Background or standard layer, and can even clone **all** layers (including Text layers or Shape layers).

To clone a region:

1. From the **Tools** toolbar's 🖈 ▾ **Clone Tools** flyout, select the 🖈 **Clone Tool**.

2. Change properties, if necessary, on the context toolbar.

3. To define the pickup origin, **Shift**-click with the tool.

4. Click again where you want to start the copy, then drag to paint the copy onto the new location. Repeat as needed. A crosshair marks the pickup point, which moves relative to your brush movements.

Drawing and editing lines and shapes

For drawing and editing lines and shapes, the **Tools** toolbar includes the following drawing tool flyouts:

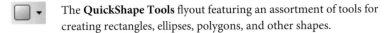 The **QuickShape Tools** flyout featuring an assortment of tools for creating rectangles, ellipses, polygons, and other shapes.

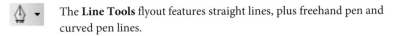 The **Line Tools** flyout features straight lines, plus freehand pen and curved pen lines.

Overview

Each of the drawing tools has its own creation and editing rules, as detailed below. Before continuing, let's cover some things that all shape objects have in common:

- Shapes have outlines known as **paths**. In a nutshell, shapes as discussed here are **filled** lines (i.e., they're closed, with colour inside). Later, we'll cover **unfilled** lines (paths) separately, and consider their special properties. The various drawing tools are all path-drawing tools, applicable to both the filled and unfilled kind of line.

- Unlike painted regions you create on **raster** (bitmap) layers, both QuickShapes and lines are **vector objects** that occupy special **shape layers**, marked with an ⑤ symbol on the Layers tab. Each shape layer includes a path thumbnail representing the shape(s) on that layer.

- A QuickShape or straight line can be drawn directly as a **shape layer**, **path** or as a filled **bitmap**. The context toolbar hosts buttons which allow you to decide how your lines and shapes are to be drawn, i.e.

  Shape Layer—create your QuickShape or line on a new shape layer or add to an existing shape layer.

  Paths—add your shape or line directly as a path rather than as a new/existing shape layer.

  Fill Bitmaps—creates a filled bitmap of the shape or straight line on any selected raster layer (e.g., the Background layer).

Curved and freehand pen lines cannot be drawn as filled bitmaps.

Creating additional shapes

Shape layers can store more than one shape, and it's up to you where additional shapes are created. This decision is made easy by use of the context toolbar when the QuickShape or line tool is selected. The toolbar displays a series of **combination buttons** which determine the layer on which the shape will be placed and the relationship the new shape will have on any existing shapes on the same layer.

New—adds the shape to a new shape layer.

Add—adds the shape to the currently selected layer.

Subtract—removes overlap region when a new shape is added over existing shapes on the currently selected layer. The new shape itself is not included.

Intersect—includes the intersection area only when a new shape is added onto existing selected shapes on the currently selected layer.

Exclude—excludes the intersection area when a new shape is added onto existing selected shapes on the currently selected layer.

> The combination buttons are also available for shapes created as paths. The buttons determine how the new shape paths interact with previously created paths.

To change the fill type, or edit its colour(s):

- Double-click the shape layer.
  OR

- Choose the Gradient Fill Tool and use the context toolbar.

  Either approach lets you update a solid colour fill, a gradient fill and/or a transparency gradient to a shape.

> A single fill is shared by all the shapes on a particular layer. (Technically the fill is a property of the layer, and the shape(s) act like a "window" that lets you see the fill.) So if you want to draw a red box and a yellow box, for example, you'll need two shape layers.

> You can also alter a shape layer's **Opacity** using the Layers tab.

Creating and editing QuickShapes

QuickShapes in PhotoPlus are pre-designed contours that let you instantly add all kinds of shapes to your image, then adjust and vary them using control handles—for innumerable possibilities!

The **QuickShape Tools** flyout lets you choose from a wide variety of commonly used shapes, including boxes, ovals, arrows, polygons, stars, and more. Each shape has its own built-in "intelligent" properties, which you can use to customize the basic shape.

QuickShapes can also be drawn as paths as described elsewhere in Using paths (see PhotoPlus Help).

To create a QuickShape :

1. Click the ⬜▾ **QuickShapes** flyout on the **Tools** Toolbar and select a shape from the flyout menu. (To choose the most recently used shape, just click the toolbar button directly.)

2. Ensure the ⊞ **Shape Layers** button is selected on the context toolbar.

3. If creating the shape on a new layer, make sure the ⬜ **New** button on the context toolbar is selected. If creating multiple shapes on the same layer, select one of the other combination buttons on the context toolbar to specify how the multiple shapes will interact (see p. 143).

4. For shapes on a new layer only, select a foreground colour for the QuickShape. Multiple shapes on the layer will adopt the layer's current colour.

5. Drag out the shape on the image. It displays as an outline; hold down the **Ctrl** key while drawing to constrain the aspect ratio.

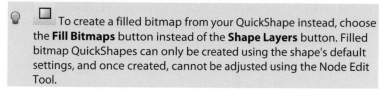

To create a filled bitmap from your QuickShape instead, choose the **Fill Bitmaps** button instead of the **Shape Layers** button. Filled bitmap QuickShapes can only be created using the shape's default settings, and once created, cannot be adjusted using the Node Edit Tool.

Each QuickShape is adjustable, so you can experiment before committing to a particular figure and edit it later—with innumerable possibilities!

If you switch to the **Node Edit Tool**, you can adjust the shape. The number of displayed "edit" control handles varies according to the shape; for example, the rectangle has just one control, the polygon has two, and the star has four.

Using the middle Quick Pentagon shape as an example:

*   Dragging the top control handle to the right will morph the shape to a hexagon, heptagon, octagon, and so on.

*   Dragging the side control handle downwards will rotate the shape anti-clockwise.

To edit a QuickShape:

1.   Click its layer or path name in the Layers or Paths tab, respectively, to select it. If on a Shape layer, make sure the layer's path thumbnail is **selected** (it has a white border; arrowed below) to allow the path to be edited with the Node Edit Tool or Shape Edit Tool, i.e.

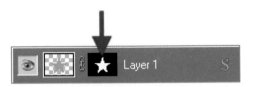

2.   From the Node Tools flyout, use either:

- The ▷ **Node Edit Tool** (**Tools** toolbar) to click on the shape and readjust any of the shape's handles.
  OR

- The 🔖 **Shape Edit Tool** to select, move, resize, and deform individual shapes.

  (If you only have one shape on a layer, you can use the **Move Tool** and **Deform Tool**.) To resize without constraint, you can drag any shape's handle; to constrain the shape's proportions, hold down the **Shift** key while dragging. To deform the shape, drag a node while the **Ctrl** key is pressed.

Creating and editing lines

Lines can be drawn by using dedicated tools from the **Tools** toolbar's Line Tools flyout.

The **Line Tool** produces an anti-aliased straight line in PhotoPlus, which is just a very thin shape. The line can be of varying **Weight** (thickness) and can be constrained to 15-degree increments, by holding down the **Shift** key as you drag.

The **Freehand Pen Tool**, as its name implies, lets you draw a squiggly line made up of consecutive line segments and nodes (each new segment starting from another's end node), which can be attached back to itself to create a closed shape. Use the **Smoothness** setting on the context toolbar to even out ragged contours automatically.

The **Pen Tool** can produce complex combination curves (and shapes) in a highly controlled way.

Each tool's supporting context toolbar lets you create the line on a shape layer or as a path. The Line Tool can also be used to create a filled bitmap directly. Additionally, combination buttons let you add the line to its own layer (or path), and can also be used to control how the new line interacts with existing shapes on the layer.

Besides being useful with QuickShapes, the Node Edit and Shape Edit tools really come into their own when editing lines.

To edit a line:

1. Click its layer name to select the layer.

2. To move, resize, scale, skew, or rotate the line, choose the [icon] **Shape Edit Tool**. This deform tool works by manipulation of the bounding box around the line—drag on a corner or edge. (For details on its use, see Deforming on p. 110.)

3. To reshape the line, choose the [icon] **Node Edit Tool**. The line consists of **line segments** and **nodes** (points where the line segments meet). You can drag one or more individual nodes, or click and drag directly on a line segment.

When you select a node, control handles for the adjacent line segments appear; each segment in the line has a control handle at either end. The selected node is drawn with a red centre, with the control handle(s) attached to the nodes by blue lines.

Any node can be one of several node types: **sharp**, **smooth**, or **symmetric**. Depending on node type, the node's control handles behave a bit differently, as you can tell with a bit of experimentation. Essentially, the node type determines the slope and curvature of each adjoining segment, and can be chosen from the context toolbar, i.e.

 **Sharp Corner** means that the segments either side of the node are completely independent so that the corner can be quite pointed.

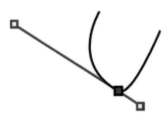 **Smooth Corner** means that the slope of the line is the same on both sides of the node, but the depth of the two joined segments can be different.

 **Symmetric Corner** nodes join line segments with the same slope and depth on both sides of the node.

To edit a node:

1. Select it with the **Node Edit Tool**.

2. Drag its control handle(s) to fine-tune the curve.

You can also use the context toolbar to define a line segment as either straight or curved.

To add a node, double-click on a line segment. To remove a selected node, press the **Delete** key.

 Use the **Straighten Line** button to make an line segment straight.

Creating and editing text

PhotoPlus makes use of two text tools, i.e.

- The **T** **Text Tool**, for entering solid text on a new layer. Use for eye-catching or subtle captioning (opposite) and titling equally.

- The **Text Selection Tool**, for creating a selection in the shape of text (for filling with unusual fills).

The Layers tab designates **text layers** with a symbol. Like shapes, solid text in PhotoPlus is **editable**: as long as it remains on a separate text layer, you can retype it or change its properties at a later date.

To create new solid text:

1. **T ▾ T** Click the **Text Tools** flyout on the **Tools** toolbar and choose the standard **Text Tool**.

2. Click on your image with the text cursor to set where you want to insert text. Then set text attributes (font, point size, bold/italic/underline, alignment, anti-alias and colour) on the Text context toolbar.
   OR

   Drag across the page to size your text according to requirements. Release the mouse button to set the point size. Then set text attributes on the Text context toolbar.

3. Type your text. The text appears on a new transparent text layer in the image. You can now use the Move Tool or other tools and commands to manipulate it, just like the contents of any layer.

To edit existing text:

1. With the text layer to be edited as the active layer, choose the standard **Text Tool** and move the mouse pointer over the text until it changes to the (I-beam) cursor.

2. Click on or drag to select areas of text—this lets you insert or overwrite selected text, respectively. Equally, you can set new text attributes (font, point size, bold/italic/underline, alignment, anti-alias, or colour) to be adopted by the selected text area—all made from the Text context toolbar.

 Fine-tune your character size and positioning by using the Character tab. If hidden, make this tab visible via **Window>Studio Tabs**.

To change text's solid colour:

1. Select all or part of any text.

2. Click the colour swatch on the context toolbar to display the Colour Selector dialog. (See Choosing colours on p. 120.)

3. Select your new colour and click **OK**.

To swap to a gradient colour:

 This applies a gradient fill to all of your text on the layer and not to selected text.

1. On the **Layers** tab, right-click the Text layer and choose **Edit Fill**.

2. Change the **Fill Type** from **Solid** to one of Linear, Radial, Conical, or Square.

3. Click on the **Fill** gradient swatch and select a preset gradient fill or create your own gradient from the dialog (see Filling a region on p. 135). The gradient fill is immediately applied to your text.

To convert any text layer to a standard layer:

*   Right-click on the layer name and choose **Rasterize** from the menu.

To create a text selection:

1. **T** ▾ 𝕋 Click the **Text Tools** flyout (**Tools** toolbar) and choose the **Text Selection Tool**.

2. Click at the location on the image where you want to begin the selection.
    OR

    Drag across the page to size your text selection according to requirements. Release the mouse button to set the point size.

3. (Optional) On the Text context toolbar, set the selection text attributes to be adopted by the new selection (e.g., the font and point size).

4. Type your text directly onto the page.

5. When you're done, click the ✅ **OK** button on the context toolbar. A selection marquee appears around the text's outline.

6. You can now cut, copy, move, modify, and of course fill the selection.

📌 Unlike solid text, the text selection doesn't occupy a separate layer.

9 Print, Export, and Share

Printing

For basic printing primarily to desktop printers, **Print Studio** offers an exciting, comprehensive, and versatile printing solution for your photos.

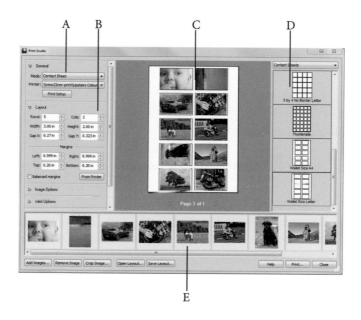

*(**A**) Print Mode, (**B**) Print Mode Options,*
*(**C**) Page Layout,(**D**) Templates, (**E**) Open Images*

The easy-to-use studio environment lets you select from a variety of print templates, each designed for either **single-** or **multi-image** printing. Multi-image printing in PhotoPlus lets you make the most of expensive photo-quality printing paper by "ganging" several images onto a single output sheet using a **print layout** or **contact sheet** template (shown above).

- **Single Image templates**
  Use for basic desktop printing of an individual image, with supporting Layout options (custom or standard print sizes, positioning, tiling, and image-to-cell fitting).

- **Print Layout templates**
  Use for multi-image standard print sizes (in portrait/landscape orientation), passport sizes, and mixed print sizes.

- **Contact Sheet templates**
  Use for multi-image template-driven thumbnail prints—great for creating labels!

✎ For any mode, you can also create your own custom template from an existing template.

✎ Currently open documents will be used for printing, although you can add more directly within Print Studio.

To print (using templates):

1. Click the 🖨 **Print** button on the **Standard** toolbar.

   The Print Studio appears.

2. (Optional) To open additional images for printing, click **Add Images**. Select a photo for addition then click **Open**. The images are added as a thumbnail to the gallery.

3. From the right-hand templates list, select a template category, e.g. Single Images (Portrait).

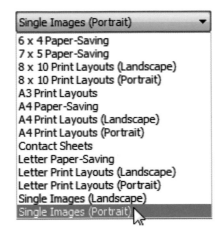

4. To insert a particular template into the central page layout region, simply click its gallery thumbnail.

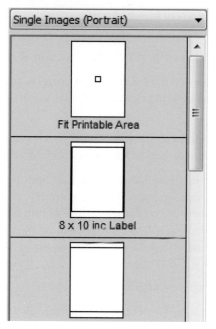

5. Depending on print mode, decide on which image(s) are to be used for printing, i.e.

    *   For **Single Image** templates, you can select a different image from the lower image gallery.

    *   For **Print Layout** templates, right-click a gallery thumbnail and select **Fill Layout with Image**. All occupied or empty cells in your layout are replaced. Alternatively, to fill an individual cell, drag a replacement image from the lower image gallery onto the "target" cell. A print layout's cells need to be manually populated; other modes will auto-populate cells.

    *   For **Contact Sheet** templates, use the **Distribution** option in **Image Options** to control image replacement.

6.   (Optional) From the left-hand pane, click the button to expand **Image Options** for sizing and rotating images (see below) in cells:

- Enable **Fit image to cell** to make the image fit within the cell boundaries.

- Enable **Fill cell with image** to scale the image to fit all of the cell.

- Check **Rotate for best fit** to make portrait images fit cells of landscape orientation (and vice versa) to make maximum use of cell space.

7.   (Optional) Check **Border** to add a border of a configurable width (use input box) and Colour (click the swatch to select colour from a dialog).

8.   (Optional) To caption your images, check **Label.** Then, from the drop-down list, select either the Date, image Filename, or Sequence number to appear under each image. For a combination of label formats, click **Modify**, add tokens to assemble a sample name, then click **OK** and the drop-down list automatically changes to Custom. See Changing file names on p. 170 for more information.

9.   Click **Print** or **Close** to save settings (but not print).

If you want to create your own layouts instead of templates you can switch print modes and customize settings for that mode.

To print using your own layouts:

1. Click the 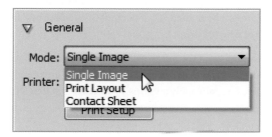 **Print** button on the **Standard** toolbar.

    The Print Studio appears.

2. From the **Mode** drop-down list, select Single Image, Print Layout, or Contact Sheet.

3. In the Layout section, select a custom or standard print **Size**.

4. (Optional) Follow image sizing and rotating instructions described above.

To store the current page layout with images:

*   Click **Save Layout** on the image gallery. PhotoPlus saves your layout exactly as is, with or without images in the cells.

To open a new layout, click **Open Layout** on the gallery.

To store the current page layout as a template without images:

*   Right-click on the right-hand template list to pop up a menu that lets you add or delete templates and categories. After creating a custom category using **Add Category** (or selecting an existing category), right-click to save your template exactly as is (without images in the cells) by using **Add Template**.

> ★ Print modes are reset each time PhotoPlus is restarted. Changes you make during a session are only "remembered" for the duration of the session.

Sizing and rotating images in cells

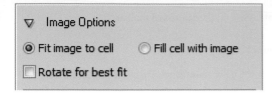

The Print dialog helps you size or rotate your image(s) to fit a cell(s) according to **Image Options** settings.

When the dialog is opened, the default settings above will be adopted. It's likely that some fine tuning might be needed, e.g. a portrait image may best be rotated to fit a cell of landscape orientation.

If further images are added from the image gallery, they will also adopt these settings. You can select an individual cell to affect the scaling or rotation on that cell only at a later time. To again apply a setting to all cells, first deselect a cell by clicking outside the grid.

Here's a visual breakdown of the different options.

Fit image to cell/Fill cell with image
These options toggle respectively between fitting the image to cell dimensions (it will scale the image width to cell width or image height to cell height) or making the image completely fill the cell, losing portions of the image from view.

Fit image to cell
enabled

Fill cell with image
enabled

Rotate for best fit
You can re-orient your image to fit cells using the **Rotate for best fit** check box—great for fitting a portrait image into landscape-oriented cells (and vice versa).

Rotate for best fit
unchecked

Rotate for best fit
checked

Cropping Images in cells

If you're looking to be more specific about which areas of your image to print, you can crop your image instead of using the above Image Options. PhotoPlus supports some sophisticated cropping options, especially the ability to crop using the image or the image's cell dimensions.

To crop an image:

1. From the dialog, select an image from the lower gallery and click **Crop Image**.

2. From the Crop Image dialog, choose an **Aspect Ratio** from the drop-down list which dictates the proportions of your crop area grid: **Unconstrained** creates a grid which can be proportioned in any way; **Cell** matches to cell dimensions; **Image** maintains image dimensions; **Custom** uses a custom constrained ratio (e.g., a square) that you define yourself in the adjacent input boxes.

Unconstrained	*Cell*	*Image*	*Custom*
		(default)	*(e.g., 1.00 x 1.00 in)*

3. Drag a crop area's corner to size your crop according to requirements, then move the grid around the image to choose the preferred image area to be cropped. To revert, click **Clear** to reset your crop grid.

4. Click **OK**.

If your image is already present in your layout then it will update automatically to reflect the new cropping applied. If it hasn't yet been used, the crop is still applied to the image in the image gallery.

 Cropping affects every instance of the image. Once applied, all images are updated.

Setting viewing options

The following global viewing options will be applied to every page.

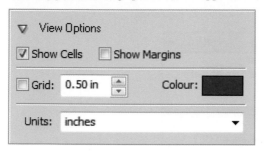

Show Cells	When checked, each cell border is displayed within which the image is placed.
Show Margins	When checked, margin guides are shown in blue.
Grid	When checked, a dot snapping grid is applied to the layout—cells will snap to the grid to aid cell positioning. Use the input box and/or Colour swatch to enter a grid interval (spacing) or pick a different grid colour via a dialog.
Units	Use the drop-down menu to select a different measurement unit used in the Layout and Image Options panes.

For professional printing, the Separations and Prepress options control CMYK colour separations and printer marks.

Printing using colour separations

The Separations and Prepress options, shown for every mode, are used for professional printing with CMYK colour separations. This process is now a less popular printing method compared to electronic PDF publishing (using PDF/X1 compliance). See PhotoPlus Help for more details.

Exporting to another file format

In many situations, you'll want to save a file to one of the standard graphics formats. In PhotoPlus, this is known as **exporting**.

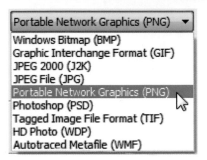

Exporting an image means converting it to a specified graphic file format other than the native PhotoPlus (.spp) format. This flattens the image, removing layer information.

Only the SPP and the Photoshop PSD formats preserves image information, such as multiple layers, masks, or image map data that would be lost in conversion to another format.

The Export process itself can be carried out by using an **Export Optimizer** where you can compare export previews for multiple file formats before export.

The Export Optimizer consists of a right-hand preview display (single, dual, or quad) and a left-hand settings region, with additional View and Zoom buttons along the bottom of the dialog. Dual and quad previews let you test and compare between different export formats in each pane—simply select a preview pane and then test various quality settings, change format-specific options or resize before going ahead with your optimized file's export—it even retains your preferred settings for each format!

Exporting images

To export an image:

1. Click **Export** from the **File** menu.

2. From the Export Optimizer dialog, use the **Options** tab to specify the **Export Area**, resampling method, file **Format**, and format-specific options such as bit depth, dithering, palette, and compression.

> ⚠ **32-bit install only:** If the **Width/Height**, **Scale** or **dpi** settings are set too high, a cross will appear over the image preview and the **Export** button will appear greyed out. You will not be able to export your photo at these settings. Reduce the specified settings to allow exporting.

3. Review your optimized image, and when you're happy with it, click **Export**. The **Close** button will instead abort the export but save any format-specific option changes made in the dialog.

4. From the Save As dialog, choose a folder and enter a file name. The export format and custom settings will be remembered for future exports. Click **OK**.

To adjust the preview display:

- To change the display scale, click the ⊖ **Zoom Out** or ⊕ **Zoom In** buttons, or rotate your mouse wheel (if available).

- When zoomed in, you can also pan around different portions of the image, by clicking and dragging on the image with the hand cursor.

- ▢ ▤ ⊞ For various preview displays, click one of the View buttons to select **Single Preview**, **Dual Preview**, or **Quad Preview**. The multi-pane (Dual and Quad) settings allow for before-and-after comparison of export settings.

To compare export settings:

1. Set the preview display to be either **Dual Preview** or **Quad Preview**.

2. Click one of the preview display panes to select it as the active pane.

3. In the Properties section, choose an export format and specific settings. Each time you make a new choice, the active pane updates to show the effect of filtering using the new settings, as well as the estimated file size.

4. To compare settings, select a different display pane and repeat the process. The Export Optimizer lets you experiment freely and evaluate the results.

To revert back to a single pane, click ▢ **Single Preview**.

To proceed with exporting:

1. Make sure the active preview pane is using the settings you want to apply to the image.

2. Click the dialog's **Export** button to display the Export dialog.

> 🖈 The dialog includes additional options for use with web images (see Slicing images and Creating image maps in PhotoPlus Help).

To preview an image in your web browser:

- Choose **Preview in Browser** from the **File** menu. PhotoPlus exports the image as a temporary file, then opens the file for preview in your web browser.

Batch processing

The batch processing feature is especially useful if you want to repeat the same operation again and again... Batch processing allows you to:

- Use Macros: uses preset or custom macros as part of the batch process.

- Change File Type: to bulk convert images to a new file type (with different file properties if needed).

- Resize Images: to resample images to various widths, heights, or resolutions (using different resampling methods).

- Change File Name: to alter the file names of images in bulk.

For any of the above, you specify separate source and destination folders as your input and output. There are several advantages to this, mainly that your original photos are not overwritten.

The **Batch** dialog, available from the **File** menu, is used to perform all of the above operations.

As a pre-requisite, you have to define a specific **Source Folder** for any batch processing operation, whether using a macro or not, or if converting photos to a different file format.

A **Destination folder** can optionally be defined, creating new files in that new location.

⚠ If you don't select a destination folder, the source files will be processed and your original files will be overwritten— exercise caution with these settings!

You may be wondering how batch processing affects photos currently loaded in PhotoPlus. PhotoPlus's batch processing only operates on source folder contents and not on the currently loaded photos themselves—so these remain unaffected. However, as a visual check, you will see each photo temporarily being loaded and converted one-by-one in the Photo window during batch processing.

 Check the output folder via Windows Explorer to ensure the results are as you expect.

Using macros

Macros (see PhotoPlus Help) can be applied to a batch process easily (via **Use Macros**). PhotoPlus doesn't differentiate between pre-recorded and recorded macros. If available, they are selected from the same **Category** and **Macro** drop-down lists equally.

Changing file type

It is possible to convert your photos into one of many different file types available in PhotoPlus (via **Change File Type**). In addition, conversion options such as bit depth, palette, dithering, compression/quality, and matte can be selected depending on the file type.

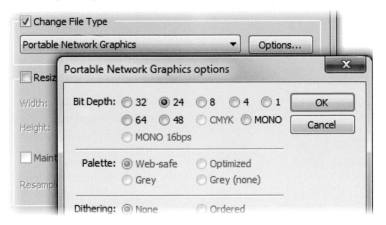

File conversions can be carried out independently or in conjunction with macros (the dialogs shown opposite converts each image to 24-bit PNG format).

Changing image size

As well as changing file formats, PhotoPlus can use batch processing to alter image sizes in bulk (using a choice of resampling methods) via **Resize Images**. Typically, this is a quick and easy way to make your images scale to a maximum image dimension (height or width) with aspect ratio maintained, to absolute image dimensions (with stretching/shrinking to fit), scale by percentage, and scale by resolution (DPI). Use for sending your digital photos via email or perhaps to publish your images online via a website.

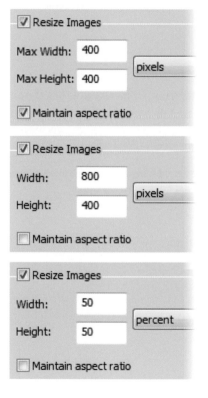

- Check **Maintain aspect ratio** then enter values for **Max Width** and **Max Height** to scale to maximum intended dimensions while preserving the image's original aspect ratio.

- With **Maintain aspect ratio** unchecked, enter values for absolute **Width** and **Height** to make images of a fixed size. As aspect ratio is not maintained, images may be stretched horizontally or vertically.

- Change the units of measurement to percent, then enter identical percentage values to scale **Width** and **Height** in proportion (maintain aspect ratio); otherwise, different values will stretch images horizontally or vertically.

- Enter a DPI value to alter the original resolution of the images.

Resampling Method

- Pick a method from the drop-down list. Use Nearest Pixel for hard-edge images, Bilinear Interpolation when shrinking photos, Bicubic Interpolation when enlarging photos, and Lanczos3 Window when best quality results are expected. The list is ordered according to processing times (fastest to slowest).

Changing file names

It is also possible to define a Destination **File Name** for the files to be processed by selecting the dialog's **Modify** button. In the **File Name Format** dialog you can select new file names that can be built up using the current date/time, document names, sequence number, or text string, individually or in combination.

 Use the sequence number to generate a separate file for every file to be converted—otherwise your first converted file will be overwritten continually!

10 Additional
Information

Contacting Serif

Contacting Serif Support

Our support mission is to provide fast, friendly technical advice and support from a team of experts.

Serif Support on the web	
Service and Support	support.serif.com
▼ Twitter	twitter.com/serifsupport
⨍ Facebook	www.facebook.com/SerifSupport

Additional Serif information

Serif on the web	
Serif website	www.serif.com
Forums	http://forums.serif.com
You Tube	http://youtube.com/serifsoftware

Main office (UK, Europe)	
Address	The Software Centre, PO Box 2000 Nottingham, NG11 7GW, UK
Phone	(0115) 914 2000
Phone (Registration)	(0800) 376 1989 +44 800 376 1989
Phone (Sales)	(0800) 376 7070 +44 800 376 7070
Phone (Service and Support)	0845 345 6770
Fax	(0115) 914 2020

North American office (US, Canada)	
Phone (Registration)	800-794-6876
Phone (Sales)	800-489-6703
Phone (Customer Service)	800-489-6720
Support	603-886-6642

For international enquiries, please contact our main office.

Credits

This User Guide, and the software described in it, is furnished under an end user License Agreement, which is included with the product. The agreement specifies the permitted and prohibited uses.

Trademarks

Serif is a registered trademark of Serif (Europe) Ltd.

PhotoPlus is a registered trademark of Serif (Europe) Ltd.

All Serif product names are trademarks of Serif (Europe) Ltd.

Microsoft, Windows and the Windows logo are registered trademarks of Microsoft Corporation. All other trademarks acknowledged.

Windows Vista and the Windows Vista Start button are trademarks or registered trademarks of Microsoft Corporation in the United States and/or other countries.

Adobe Photoshop is a registered trademark of Adobe Systems Incorporated in the United States and/or other countries.

Copyrights

11 Index